bonsai

bonsai

Peter Chan

Skyhorse Publishing

Skyhorse Publishing books may be purchased in bulk at special discounts for sales promotion, corporate gifts, fund-raising, or educational purposes. Special editions can also be created to specifications. For details, contact the Special Sales Department, Skyhorse Publishing, 307 West 36th Street, 11th Floor, New York, NY 10018 or info@skyhorsepublishing.com.

Skyhorse® and Skyhorse Publishing® are registered trademarks of Skyhorse Publishing, Inc. ®, a Delaware corporation.

This book produced by Quantum Publishing Ltd, 6 Blundell Street, London N7 9BH.

www.skyhorsepublishing.com

10 9 8 7 6

Library of Congress Cataloging-in-Publication Data is available on file.

ISBN: 978-1-62914-168-8

Printed in China

CONTENTS

The two words "bon sai'" literally translated, mean a potted tree. However, bonsai also denotes the cultivation of trees in pots. The characters are the same in both Chinese and Japanese.

INTRODUCTION

What is bonsai?

Bonsai is simply the art and science of growing miniature trees and shrubs in decorative pots. And yet, there is so much mystique surrounding its practice that many people, including those with green fingers, are put off by what appears to be a very complicated and lengthy process. However, if you were to take the trouble to delve a little deeper you would soon discover that ordinary horticultural principles are involved and that bonsai is really no more than an extension of everyday gardening. The only difference is that the trees and pots have a particular aesthetic quality about them, both as individuals in their own right and as ensembles.

Misconceptions about bonsai

As with all human endeavors, knowledge is the key that unlocks everything. This is as true of bonsai as it is of mathematics. Bonsai need not be shrouded in mystery, and the Japanese and Chinese need not have the monopoly of wisdom in this area. Because of the mystique which has grown up over the years around bonsai, many misconceptions and myths have gained credence. A common myth is that the practice of bonsai is cruel to trees. Those who think this imagine that the dwarfing process inflicts great pain on the tree. This widespread misconception has probably been fostered by memories of the ancient Chinese custom of foot binding in which the feet of young girls were prevented from growing by having tight bandaging from a very early age. This was indeed a cruel custom which has, of course, long been banned in China. However, people in the West still associate this practice with the dwarfing technique used in bonsai, for obvious reasons. Both processes restrict growth and somehow the dwarfing of trees by branch and root pruning is thought to be equally cruel. Of course anyone who is a gardener will know that branch and root pruning are an essential element in gardening. Roses, hedges, and even fruit trees need to be pruned from time to time. So with bonsai. Root pruning is necessary and is widely practised by gardeners and nurserymen the world over. Most gardeners will know that root pruning stimulates the development of fibrous roots. The undercutting of young trees and shrubs is standard horticultural practice and the development of containerized shrubs for the garden center trade is a vivid example of why root pruning is so essential. Yet no one would argue that root and branch pruning as practised in the nursery trade is cruel to the shrubs and trees. The fact that bonsai live to a great old age suggests that they receive better treatment and care than their counterparts in the wild.

The accusation that bonsai is cruel to trees does not really hold.

Another, even stranger, misconception which has gained credence over the years is that a bonsai is first grown from seed planted in a grapefruit skin, and that as the roots grow through the skin they are clipped or singed to keep the tree dwarfed. Again, nothing could be further from the truth. It is hard to imagine how a seed could develop into a tree in a grapefruit skin without the skin rotting and getting moldy. No one knows how this particular myth developed but it is one which is often heard.

Bonsai defined

So far I have described only what a bonsai is not. But what is a bonsai? A bonsai, or miniature tree, has sometimes been described by cynics as a horticultural pygmy with delusions of grandeur. That may be so, but literally translated, the two Chinese words *bon-sai*, which incidentally are the same in the Japanese language, mean a potted tree. However, merely having a tree in a pot does not necessarily make it a bonsai. A bonsai is an artistic replica of a natural tree in miniature form. It exists only in a pot or container. It is essentially a work of art and is produced by man through expert care and manipulation of natural plant material. It is above all a picture or illusion of a real tree.

An art form

Bonsai is an art form. Like any of the other visual arts such as painting or sculpture, it has all the essential aesthetic elements of composition, balance, perspective, depth, texture, color and so on. The analogy of bonsai with painting in general, and landscape painting in particular, is especially appropriate. The objectives both in landscape painting and in bonsai are the same, in each case to create on a reduced scale what one observes in nature. Just as in painting, where the artist tries to reproduce on a small piece of canvas a vast panorama extending several miles or kilometres—so in bonsai you seek to create a miniature tree no more than a yard high from something which in nature would normally grow to 100 feet (30 meters) or more. In fact, there is a variant of bonsai practised by the Chinese called *pen-jing* or potted landscape. The Japanese equivalent of this is *sai-kei* or tray scenery. In this form of bonsai, the object is to create scenery with real live plant material in three-dimensional form.

Over the centuries, the technique of growing trees in pots has developed into a highly sophisticated art form. Bonsai is not simply growing healthy trees in pots. The trees must be beautiful in their own right. The pot and the tree together must form a unified whole. Some bonsai live to a great age; in Japan

The young Scots pine seedling on the left is not much to look at in its black plastic flower pot. However, it does have some potential as a bonsai. The same tree, when transplanted into a proper bonsai pot, takes on an altogether different character. But it cannot really be called a bonsai yet. Given the right care and attention, this tree could become a handsome bonsai in a few years' time.

today, there are bonsai which are estimated to be 500 to 700 years old. Their recorded history as bonsai can certainly be traced back over at least the last three hundred years. However, age is not the most important factor—the beauty of the tree is the major consideration.

Continuing with the analogy of painting, mention must be made of bonsai masterpieces. Just as there are masterpieces in painting, so in bonsai the really beautiful specimens of these dwarf trees are regarded as masterpieces in their own right. These bonsai masterpieces are invariably very ancient trees in excess of two hundred years old and they are, not surprisingly, held in very high esteem. Their value is inestimable as they are living antiques. But a specimen bonsai tree is different from a famous painting or sculpture in one important respect. A painting or sculpture is a finished work of art, whereas a bonsai masterpiece is dynamic, always evolving and never finished as such. It needs to be continually kept in tip-top condition if it is to retain its beauty and fame. The work of a bonsai artist is therefore never complete. The responsibility is a continuing one and is very often carried over from one generation to the next.

Few people fail to be fascinated by these miniature trees; some are attracted by the age of specimens, others by their sheer beauty. Most people, of course, are simply intrigued by the curiosity of miniaturization, many miss the whole point of bonsai if they look no further than the horticultural aspect of this pastime. Bonsai is first and foremost an art form. A good bonsai is one which resembles a real tree which can be anything from a few inches to a yard high. Size and age are not the most important factors. What matters is the visual impact on the person looking at the tree: it must express the beauty and majesty of a tree growing in its natural environment. If it looks like a real tree, then the bonsai artist will have succeeded, but it is important to remember that in bonsai one is creating an image or an illusion; unlike Coca Cola a bonsai is not "the real thing". The bonsai artist can create this illusion by all manner of means. But the end product must be aesthetically pleasing, delighting both the eye and the soul!

Right: Japanese larch collected from the wild fifteen years ago. It was found growing in a rock face and the tree was planted in this fashion to recreate the original setting. It is now 28 inches high and has been estimated to be about fifty years old. The tree bears cones every year. Here it is shown in its beautiful fall color; like all larches, it makes an extremely handsome bonsai. They have beautiful apple-green leaves in the spring and, in the fall, they turn a lovely golden-yellow color. They are extremely hardy, tolerate drought well, and need little or no winter protection. This is not just a tree in a pot—it is very much a work of art.

Below: Detail of the larch on page 11. This tree was originally planted in a cleft of the large piece of rock. The trunk has thickened considerably over the years and in the process has split the rock.

Characteristics of a good bonsai

A good bonsai must have an impressive and characterful trunk. It need not necessarily be thick in every case, but it should be attractive to look at. The trunk should rise gradually out of its pot from a good radial root system. It should preferably have buttress roots, and taper gradually all the way up to the top. The branches should be evenly distributed around the trunk, and the front of the tree should be exposed to view as much as possible. There should be slightly fewer branches at the front than at the rear so that the observer will have a good impression of depth and perspective. The branches too should taper all the way up to the crown of the tree and the overall shape should be conical in form. The bark of the trunk should have interesting color and texture, as should the foliage. The foliage should, of course, be in prime condition at all times; there should be no scorch marks left by strong wind or harsh sunshine. It should have the appropriate color for the time of year if it is a deciduous tree, and it should look generally healthy and be free from disease. The tree must be planted in precisely the correct position in the pot and the pot itself must be in harmony with the composition of the tree as a whole. The pot and the tree must complement each other because only then will the picture they create please the eye.

This is what a good bonsai ought to look like and one should be able to distinguish a bad bonsai from a good one. Unfortunately, there are many inferior bonsai which are sold by unscrupulous dealers today. They are passed off as genuine bonsai. These "bonsai" are often nothing more than young two or three-year-old seedlings or cuttings in little round dishes. They will have had hardly any training whatsoever and are merely plants in plastic or ceramic bowls. The chances are that these bowls are not even proper bonsai pots. These little trees may have the potential of becoming good bonsai in years to come, given proper training and grooming, but it would be quite wrong to call them real bonsai trees. You should therefore beware of such products and follow instead one of the surer methods recommended in the next chapter.

Bonsai as a hobby

Bonsai is a fascinating hobby. In the West, interest in this pastime has mushroomed in the last thirty years. It was not very long ago that these strange little trees were regarded purely as curiosities. Today, the bonsai following is worldwide. People seem to be attracted by them because they are beautiful living objects. There is also a certain charm about them being small and yet so old.

The growth of interest in bonsai is part of the increased interest in other Asian arts such as judo, karate, ikebana, and even cooking. Travel and communication have undoubtedly helped to spread the knowledge of these arts, but the real reason why Westerners have become interested in bonsai is because they wish to have contact with nature and create beautiful things. What could be more beautiful than a tree less than a yard high but perfect in every other respect?

A further very good reason for the increase in popularity of bonsai is that the pastime is a very restful one. Simply looking at a few attractive bonsai can restore one's inner calm and tranquility.

Bonsai knows no racial, cultural, religious or even class barriers. It has a following in almost every country today, and it attracts people from every stratum of society. Club memberships may include among their numbers plumbers, solicitors, artists, engineers, lorry drivers and doctors. It is amazing how bonsai can transcend the usual barriers of class and social status. The hobby has a unifying influence in society and one hopes that peace and harmony will be promoted as this pastime grows in popularity.

What does the hobby entail?

To the uninitiated, bonsai may be steeped in mystery, but to the person who has some knowledge of the subject, it need not be so daunting. It is a logical extension of ordinary gardening practice applied to trees and shrubs. Bonsai is, after all, the cultivation of trees and shrubs in pots. If one has grown trees and plants successfully in pots or window boxes, then one is almost half way there. To be successful at bonsai, however, it is not enough to be a good horticulturalist; an artistic aptitude is necessary too. A bonsai may be just a "potted tree", but it is really much more than that. It is said that "a tree in a pot is a tree in a pot—but a bonsai is a work of art". Bonsai must therefore transcend horticulture. A good grasp of horticultural principles is a prerequisite for successful bonsai growing, but it is not the entire substance of bonsai. Indeed, it is more important to be an artist than a horticulturalist in this game. A keen eye for beauty is more important than green fingers.

Having said that, there are certain tricks and secrets to be learnt which will help the reader acquire the essential skills of the art of bonsai fairly painlessly. These are the subject of the following chapters. A bonsai basically needs watering, feeding and pruning. If these three requirements are met, then the result is success. If they are not, then the tree will cease to be a bonsai. It might even die! I hope that this book will simplify the art and science of bonsai and give the reader endless years of pleasure in growing beautiful miniature trees.

Left: This exquisite Japanese mountain maple (*Acer palmatum*) is probably the finest specimen of maple bonsai outside Japan. It was imported from Japan in the mid 1960s and is estimated to be about 100 years old. Grown in the split trunk style, it measures 80 cm high and 80 cm wide. The fall color is spectacular but the tree is perhaps more elegant without its leaves than when it has its full canopy of foliage.

Right: This needle juniper (*Juniperus rigida*) is the largest and oldest bonsai in my collection. It was imported from Japan into the UK about 1946. It is a magnificent tree with lots of beautiful driftwood. The trunk is 25 cm in diameter at soil level. It is 90 cm high and 120 cm wide. Like most other exquisite specimen bonsai, this particular tree must have been collected from a wild mountainous region many, many years ago

Above: An example of *pen-jing* or Chinese potted landscape, an extremely popular art form in China. The scene here is of men fishing under some high cliffs. I created this composition using tufa rock and little cotoneasters. The tray, or water basin, is a metre long and the boats just under 5 cm. The fishermen are barely a centimetre high.

Detail of the same tree showing the driftwood which is its particular attraction. Only about a fifth of the trunk is still alive, but the tree is generally very healthy. The driftwood is treated with lime sulfur twice a year: once in the early summer and later on in mid-summer. This serves to preserve the wood from decay.

The Chinese have always loved plants and flowers. This
ancient manuscript depicts a family with artistic plant
arrangements.

CHAPTER 2

HISTORICAL ORIGINS

A spectacular view of Chinese
mountains. Note how the trees grow
out of the cliffs and rock faces.

It is commonly imagined that bonsai originated in Japan; this is
not the case. Bonsai has its origins in China. The Chinese were
the first to practise the cultivation of trees and shrubs in
ceramic flower pots. There is evidence that as far back as AD 200
the Chinese were already growing potted plants as part of their
everyday gardening. The Chinese have a very long tradition of
gardening. They were probably one of the earliest civilizations,
together with the e.g.yptians and Persians, to have found the
time to practise this sophisticated art. Indeed one of the marks
of an advanced civilization is its ability to create beautiful
gardens. The earliest Chinese gardens can be traced back to
the Shang Dynasty (sixteenth to the eleventh centuries BC).

People have often wondered why the e.g.yptians and Persians
never developed bonsai. This was probably because e.g.yptian
and Persian garden art was quite unlike Chinese garden art.
There are a number of reasons for this. The most important is
the fact that China, unlike e.g.ypt and Persia, had a wealth of
indigenous plants. In the temperate world, China has the
greatest variety of flora. Its natural environment was extremely
beautiful. The mountains, hills and plains were simply
breathtaking. They still are today. It is within this advantageous
setting that the Chinese developed gardens, and the Chinese
could not help but create a style of gardening which reflected
the natural environment they found around them. The other
two races, on the other hand, lived in a rather drier
environment, and it was therefore understandable that their
gardens should shut out the natural environment and create a
different fantasy world altogether.

The Chinese created in their gardens a world which was
almost an exact copy of nature. It is not difficult to imagine an
early Chinese garden filled with such lovely plants as forsythia,
camellia, azalea, rhododendron, roses, moutan (tree paeony),
crape myrtle and so on. These plants are all indigenous to
China and were brought back to Europe by the famous plant
hunters of the eighteenth and nineteenth centuries.

The Chinese were therefore one of the earliest peoples to
appreciate the natural beauty which they found around them.
Nature provided all the guidelines they needed for the
development of their aesthetic sensibilities. That is why the
Chinese garden is noted for its "natural" style and contrived
informality. The influence of the flora was all-pervasive and it is
reflected over and over again in all the major Chinese art forms
ie painting, poetry, sculpture and even music. It is said that in
no other civilization have flowers and plants played such a
major role as they have in Chinese art. The Chinese have
written volumes throughout the ages on horticulture. It is in
these writings that we learn of the transplanting of fully grown
trees as far back as AD 500, and the use of air-layering as a
method of propagation at about the same time.

The informality of the Chinese garden, which is in stark
contrast to the orderliness of Chinese architecture, has always
intrigued Western scholars. But there is a logical explanation

for this. The Chinese are essentially a pragmatic race. They choose one set of principles when it suits them and another when it does not. There is also a philosophical basis to this approach. To the Chinese, geometric patterns are reserved for those areas which express human relationships. When it comes to our relationship with the natural world, they believe that things are best if they are allowed to run their natural course. This may smack of laissez-faire, but it has a philosophical basis. The Chinese have successfully adapted both Confucian and Taoist teachings in their everyday living. Thus their houses reflected Confucian principles while their gardens followed Taoist lines. The former regulated human and societal relationships, the latter, the human relationship with the environment. What Chinese gardeners practised 2,000 years ago environmentalists today are still trying to achieve. Gardening also provided the Chinese with the opportunity of releasing their creative energies, which to a certain extent was denied them in architecture.

Chinese imperial gardens

The Chinese garden, not unlike those of other civilizations, has its origins in imperial gardens. Gardening could flourish only under royal patronage. With their great wealth, the Chinese emperors created magnificent gardens on a colossal scale. Chinese historical writings record details of many of these fine imperial gardens. They often covered areas as large as some of the major cities of the modern world. These imperial gardens included hills, mountains and huge man-made lakes. For the Chinese emperors the size and majesty of their gardens was a reflection of their own splendour and power. Their gardens were intended to be symbols of the empire In microcosm. They were designed in such a way that miniature hills, mountains, streams and lakes symbolized the real hills, mountains, streams and lakes which existed in the kingdom. The *Sek-San* (or mountains made from rock) which the Chinese still make today, are relics of that ancient tradition.

Mountains in Chinese art

At this point, mention must be made of mountains, because mountains had particular symbolic significance. They were considered absolutely essential if the imperial gardens were to be true representations of the Chinese kingdom. In China, the great mountains are quite breathtaking. They were believed to be the repositories of the energy of the universe and regarded with the greatest awe. This respect for mountains led to the veneration and worship of rocks which reached a peak in the

Ancient Chinese silk embroidery depicting the Eight Immortals. This scroll has been in my family for nearly a century.

Tang dynasty (AD 600-900). No other race has adored the beauty and splendour of mountains as the Chinese have. Mountains have always appealed to them from ancient times. Again this is due partly to Taoism. Mountains evoke a sense of the remote, the eternal, and the all-powerful, and this is how the Taoists viewed man's relationship with the universe.

As far back as the fifth century BC, there are records of Chinese poets and scholars making special trips into the mountains for inspiration. Some have described their experiences as a mixture of pleasure and fear. Others have even compared the experience to a burning sexual passion. The ancient Chinese artists do not exaggerate when they paint mountain cliffs rising directly from the plains, and summits shrouded in mist floating above seemingly horizonless lakes. Such breathtaking scenery can still be seen in China today. Thus, impressionism and reality are confirmed in a common visual experience. It is in the context of this romantic setting that the Chinese belief in the "Immortals" or *Hsien* has

Detail of Chinese style bonsai showing the old gnarled and twisted trunks which were so greatly loved by the Taoists. The tree is a *Vitex chinensis* or chaste tree, imported from western China into the UK in 1980. It is reputed to be well over 100 years old, and blooms regularly each summer. The soft mauve flowers are a striking contrast to the rugged-looking trunk. This bonsai is 55 cm high and 65 cm wide.

developed. There are by tradition eight Immortals (called the *PartHsien*) and they were believed to have lived in the mountains. They occasionally visited people on earth, but were seldom seen. It is not surprising therefore that the mountains and the Immortals became the particular obsession of the Taoists. It is no secret that they were obsessed with immortality. The Chinese concept of immortality was more down-to-earth and pragmatic than that of the Christian. For the Chinese, immortality meant a modest extension of one's earthly life—a couple of hundred years perhaps. The Christian, on the other hand, thinks of immortality in terms of infinity in the afterlife. The Taoists played an important part in the development of bonsai because in the course of their researches into plants and minerals, which were motivated by the hope of discovering the elixir of life, they accumulated a vast fund of knowledge of natural medicine. For instance, they discovered a mushroom which was supposed to have life-prolonging properties (not unlike some of the mushrooms which are supposed today to produce hallucinatory effects). In ancient Chinese paintings, Taoist priests are often shown carrying the sacred mushroom and a little replica of a sacred mountain. These miniature symbols are of immense significance because the Taoists believed that by miniaturizing an object they could concentrate and manipulate all its magical qualities. Miniaturization and dwarfing were therefore very much to do with practical magic and the search for immortality. The Taoists dwarfed and extended the lives of trees by slowing the rise of sap just as they slowed their own pulse and breathing in their, attempts to extend human life. In a sense, the old twisted trunks of the trees were a reflection of the old and twisted shapes of the Taoists themselves. It was not just the Taoist priests who dabbled in the metaphysical; the mandarins and scholars also dabbled in this form of magic. One of the earliest recorded practitioners of bonsai was a Chinese mandarin in the fourth century AD called Tong Kwo Ming who forsook his profession to grow potted chrysanthemums. This is not surprising because mandarins fled the imperial court in droves during the fourth and sixth centuries AD because it had become so utterly corrupt. The scholars often went off for long periods into the mountains to distance themselves from worldly affairs where they could indulge in the making of simple gardens using borrowed scenery.

These scholars were known as "literati" and they had a most profound influence on Chinese art in general and on bonsai in particular. The "literati style" in bonsai is considered by connoisseurs of the art as the most expressive and artistic of all bonsai styles and its origin can be traced directly to this group of artists who forsook worldly pleasures for the contemplative life.

The literati were a very select group of people in China, scholars and artists of the highest calibre who admitted into their circle only those who met their very stringent standards.

They were essentially calligraphers because they were first and foremost literary scholars and also included accomplished poets and painters.

Chinese calligraphy demands a sophisticated aesthetic sense and the literati had a particularly highly developed sense of composition and balance. The calligrapher exploited all the possibilities of his medium; the control of brush, paper, and ink density were some of the subtle techniques used in creating their works of art. It was the literati who first painted trees and mountains in that very distinctive cryptic style, where the composition was achieved with the minimum use of brush strokes. Their paintings captivated the ordinary Chinese, and the style is still very popular today. Their style of depicting trees very quickly influenced the development of bonsai and potted scenery. Just as Chinese garden art was influenced heavily by Chinese painting, so in the same way Chinese bonsai evolved almost entirely from the painting of the literati. It was never the other way round—i.e.Chinese gardens did not determine the style of Chinese painting and Chinese bonsai did not determine the style of literati. It is because of this that literati bonsai bear only slight resemblance to trees seen in real life. They are artistic impressions of trees, illusions if you like! This is precisely what bonsai is about.

Chinese scroll paintings dating back to around AD 600 were already depicting, miniature trees in beautiful ceramic pots. These trees were very similar to Chinese bonsai grown today. Bonsai gradually spread to other parts of the Orient and by the eleventh or twelfth century, had gained a foothold in Japan. Bonsai was introduced to the Japanese by Chinese Buddhist monks. Today the Japanese are the undisputed masters of the art. They have adapted the art form and surpassed the Chinese who originally invented it. Bonsai remains popular in China today despite the upheaval of the Cultural Revolution of the 1960s. The Chinese have managed to preserve this traditional art form and have now begun to take a fresh interest in it.

The Chinese and Japanese styles of bonsai differ quite significantly. The Chinese have their own particular brand of bonsai. They are very good at creating potted landscapes but not as good as the Japanese at creating individual specimen trees. Although this is a purely personal view, many bonsai enthusiasts in the West feel the same way. The Japanese style is more naturalistic and greater attention is paid to detail and overall presentation. With the liberalization of China in the last few years, those who have had the privilege of travelling in that country have nothing but the highest praise for the distinctiveness of Chinese bonsai. It is true that the Chinese have a different philosophical and stylistic approach, perhaps not entirely to the liking of those who are more accustomed to seeing Japanese bonsai. However, these are early days and we might yet grow to appreciate the original approach to the art with its long and rich traditions stretching back nearly 3,000 years.

An example of Chinese style rock planting I created. The rock is carboniferous limestone collected in Wales. The rock is 40 cm high, planted with dwarf bamboo and sedum in a Chinese pot.

Another fine view of mountains in China and an obvious
source of inspiration for bonsai artists.

STARTING OFF

"The longest journey begins with the first step" is an old Chinese proverb. This is certainly true of bonsai. To become proficient in the art, i.e. to become a bonsai master or expert, you must be prepared to embark on a long journey of discovery. This journey has no end because there is no such thing as ultimate perfection. What you can hope to achieve is something approaching it. The journey will, however, be a most rewarding and satisfying experience, and the traveler will enjoy every moment of it.

There is as much pleasure, for instance, in creating bonsai from young seedlings which you have grown youself, as there is from shaping gnarled old material collected from the mountains. Both are equally satisfying. Most enthusiasts will remember the thrill of owning or making their first bonsai. This experience is not unlike falling in love for the first time! There will, of course, be other pleasurable experiences in life, such as marriage, children, grandchildren, and so on. The bonsai journey is no different. The important thing is to enjoy the hobby as it unfolds day by day.

People often make the excuse that they are too old to start in bonsai because they will never see the tree grow to its full glory. They presumably imagine that age is the only criterion which matters, and that all bonsai must be grown from seed. Nothing could be further from the truth. It is never too late to get started. If you wish to produce bonsai from seedlings or cuttings, extremely good specimens can be produced in as little as three years. The easiest way to get started in bonsai is, of course, to buy a ready-made tree from one of the specialist bonsai nurseries. It is possible to buy anything from a two-year old tree to another which might be as much as two-hundred years old.

The quality of the tree will depend on how much you are prepared to spend on it. It would be unwise for someone who has no experience of bonsai whatsoever to start with an extremely valuable old specimen: There is always the risk that the owner might not be able to give the tree the proper attention needed to maintain it in prime condition. There is the risk, too, of killing the tree.

Bonsai can also be created from garden center material. Expertise is needed, of course, and must be prepared to learn the basic skills needed to keep the tree alive and healthy. These can be acquired almost exclusively by reading books, as I did when I started bonsai eighteen years ago. Tips can often be picked up by talking to experts, or by joining a good bonsai club. In the last analysis, there is nothing like doing it yourself. Mistakes may occur, but they are all part of the fun of bonsai. As in any other learning process, mistakes are the necessary price paid for experience and success. There is no mystique to bonsai. It really is quite easy! If you have already grown shrubs and trees in pots and tubs, you are halfway to becoming a bonsai expert!

There are essentially six basic ways of getting started in bonsai. These are:

1 Growing from seed
2 Propagation from cuttings, grafting, or air-layering
3 Using young nursery or garden center trees
4 Using more mature commercial trees
5 Using collected material found in the wild
6 Buying ready-made bonsai

Growing from seed

There has been a boom, in recent years, in the sale of "bonsai seeds". There is, of course, no such thing as bonsai seed. While it is true that certain species of trees are natural dwarfs—dwarf conifers are a good example—bonsai trees do not grow from bonsai seeds.

Trees are made into bonsai by special pruning and training techniques. Beware of advertisements selling "bonsai seed". These are usually ordinary seeds which are sold at a premium by unscrupulous dealers who wish to exploit the special image of bonsai. The correct description is "tree seeds suitable for growing as bonsai". You should not really have to pay extortionate prices for them.

Certain varieties of trees grow particularly easily from seed. Others of course are more difficult. Japanese maples, trident maples, black pine, Scots pine, zelkovas, beech, almond, horse chestnut, crab apple, quince, and larch are easy subjects. Hinoki cypress, white pine, hornbeam, and needle juniper are some of the varieties slightly more difficult to germinate.

The ability of tree seeds to germinate depends on a number of factors: The quality of the seed, its origin, the season and manner of its collection and storage and finally, its "germination capacity". Some seeds have the additional complication of dormancy. This is nature's way of protecting the seed during the winter so that it can awake from its sleep in the following spring ready to grow into a proper tree.

Premature germination, e.g. fall germination in a cool temperate region would be futile because the young seedling would soon succumb to the first winter frosts. Varieties of seed that exhibit dormancy need to be stimulated into growth by a number of special methods, the most common of which is a process called stratification. This is a process in which the seeds are mixed with sand and left in a specially prepared pit through the winter. The effect of alternate freezing and thawing by frost and snow eventually breaks the seeds' dormancy.

Stratification can also be achieved artificially with the help of a domestic refrigerator. In this process, the seed is first soaked in water for about six hours, and then put in a damp plastic bag at room temperature for a couple of days. Starting at the

These seeds were helped to germinate by refrigeration for about a month. Fresh seeds are obviously most reliable.

The ideal seed sowing compost is a mixture of equal parts of sphagnum moss peat and sharp sand.

Thoroughly mix the peat and sand until the compost is a homogeneous mixture.

When the mixture has been prepared, lightly tamp it down with a block of wood so that the surface of the compost is fairly level.

Once the surface of the compost is reasonably level, the seeds may be sown over this.

Take a few seeds and scatter them evenly over the surface of the compost. A seed tray measuring 14 by 8 inches could take up to two hundred seeds.

Cover the seeds with the compost to a depth of two or three times the thickness of the seed. In practice, a layer of 0.5 cm is sufficient.

Most seeds germinate in two to four weeks. These Black pine seedlings are four months old.

bottom of a refrigerator where the temperature should be about 40°F (4°C), it should be gradually moved up over a period of about two weeks, to higher shelves, where the temperature should be about 34°F (1°C). It must then be gradually moved back to the lower part of the refrigerator over a second two-week period after which it will be ready for sowing. Stratification is therefore a gradual process. This method should work for most varieties of seeds that exhibit dormancy, although it must be emphasized that it is not the only way of overcoming dormancy.

It is sometimes useful to put seeds which have a hard coating or outer surface in to a freezer or the freezing compartment of a refrigerator, for a short while but not exceeding two or three days at most. Remember that the seeds' introduction into the freezer or freezing compartment should be done gradually, i.e. they should be taken from the warmest part of the refrigerator to the coldest part, and then into the freezer. The thawing out can be done in a similar manner.

Dormancy is a very complex subject because of the many different forms. The two most common forms are physical

Given the right conditions, seedlings develop very rapidly into sturdy little trees. These are mostly two to three years old. Some of them already have potential as bonsai. If larger trees are wanted seedlings at this stage should be potted on into larger containers or even planted in the ground.

dormancy and exogenous dormancy. Physical dormancy is due to the nature of the covering of the seed. Certain seeds have a very tough coating which needs to be broken down before germination can begin. Endogenous dormancy is due to the inherent nature of the seed embryo itself. To complicate matters further, there is yet another type of dormancy called morphological dormancy which is due to incomplete embryo development. It may therefore be of some comfort to the reader to know that when a seed fails to germinate it could be due to a large number of factors which are completely outside his control. A useful tip to remember is that when the temperature gets too high, as in a greenhouse during late spring or early summer, some seeds may become dormant again and therefore fail to germinate. A number of pine seeds tend to behave in this manner. That is why pine seeds will germinate quite freely until early summer, but with the onset of higher temperatures in a greenhouse in mid-summer they may fail to germinate altogether. This fact is not always appreciated by many gardeners.

The best time to sow tree seeds is in spring. Fill an ordinary plastic seed tray with a 1:1 mix of peat and sand. Medium-grade sphagnum moss and washed sharp sand are ideal. Alternatively, use a ready-mixed seed sowing compost or a soil-less seed growing compost which is peat-based. Fill the seed tray to half its depth with compost, press it down lightly, and then sprinkle the seed evenly over the surface. Next, cover the seed with a further sprinkling of compost to a depth of about two to three times the thickness of the seed. Thus, if the seed is $\frac{1}{8}$ in (3mm) in diameter, cover the seeds to a depth of $\frac{1}{4}$-$\frac{3}{8}$ in (6-9 mm). Finally, sprinkle over the top of this a fine layer of sharp sand or grit to keep the seeds weighted down. Keep the compost moist at all times but never soaking wet. A temperature of about 50-60°F (10-15°C) is ideal for germination and this makes the environment of an ordinary kitchen a very suitable place in which to keep the seed trays. If you have a cool or heated greenhouse so much the better. A heated propagator would, of course, be ideal. It is advisable to water the seeds with a solution of weak Bordeaux mixture or Cheshunt compound to prevent "damping off". At the right temperature the seeds should begin to sprout in about two to four weeks time. Leave the seedlings in the seed tray until the first pair of proper leaves develops. These should not be confused with the cotyledons. At this stage the seedlings can be pricked off and planted into individual $1\frac{1}{2}$ in (4 cm) peat or plastic pots. When transplanting the seedlings, use a seed sowing compost and not a compost for potting up, as the fertilizer strength of ordinary potting compost might be a bit too much for the young seedlings. If you normally mix your own compost, add a small quantity of base fertilizer so that the young seedlings have some nutrients to sustain their growth in the early period. Too much fertilizer would, of course, be detrimental. It will not be necessary to fertilize the seedlings for the first four or five weeks after transplanting, but thereafter feed them with a dilute solution of liquid fertilizer. Any of the proprietary liquid fertilizers will do. In the first growing season seedlings could grow 6-36 in (15-90 cm) high depending on the species of the tree. If the seedlings have been sown rather late, i.e. after mid-summer, it may be advisable to leave them in the seed tray to overwinter rather than to pot them individually in the fall. Potting up can be done in the following spring. Seedlings should be allowed to grow freely for the first two or three years before any shaping or training is done. During this period, the seedlings can be transplanted gradually into larger pots or, if you have a nursery bed set aside for young seedlings, they could make rapid growth in the ground. Some seedlings can grow as much as 5-6 ft (1.5-1.8 m) in the first two to three years and the stem could develop to $\frac{1}{2}$ or $\frac{3}{4}$ in (or 2cm) in diameter.

Generally speaking, seedlings are not always as vigorous as this; they will probably be about the thickness of a pencil after three years growth. Trees at this stage are ideal for training into bonsai. The seedling should be cut back to 6 to 9 in (15 to 23 cm) and the trunk wired into the desired basic shape. Do not worry too much about the branches at this stage as they can always be removed later on. The more numerous the branches, the stronger the young tree will be. Try to encourage branches to grow evenly around the trunk from fairly low down.

If the object at this stage is to create a mame or miniature size bonsai, the seedling should be kept under 6 in (15 cm) high. The "lazy S" is a classic bonsai shape and is very popular and attractive for these miniature size bonsai. The tap root of the seedling should be removed so as to encourage the development of side roots and a fibrous root system. Put the young seedling into a *mame* pot using the same basic seed-sowing compost as for potting up seedlings.

If a slightly larger size bonsai is desired, then the seedling should be allowed to grow progressively larger by growing it on in a larger pot at each repotting. Growing bonsai from seed can be a very satisfying and rewarding process because one sees the tree at every stage of development. It is also, contrary to popular belief, a relatively quick process. Often a very credible looking bonsai can be produced in as little as six or seven years. A tree of this age could even have a trunk as thick as 1 in (2.5 cm) depending on how it had been grown. Hornbeams and trident maples are particularly rapid growers.

Bonsai from cuttings, grafts, and air-layerings

Bonsai can also be developed from cuttings. The taking of cuttings is really quite simple if one knows precisely what to

do. For those with a green thumb this presents no problem, but for the vast majority of people the process is very much a hit-and-miss affair. Success is seldom consistent. However, there is no reason why this method, used with care, should not be as successful as raising trees from seed.

As in the case of seeds, there are certain varieties of trees and plants which are easier to propagate from cuttings than others. Willow, poplar, forsythia, quince, rose, and certain juniper species are very easy subjects to strike from cuttings, while others, including Japanese white pine, the rarer Japanese maples, spruces, larches, and cedars can be extremely difficult, if not impossible.

There are basically two types of cuttings, soft-wood and hard-wood cuttings. Soft-wood cuttings are taken from shoots produced in the current growing season that have not yet turned woody. They are usually taken in early mid-summer from growth that started in spring. Hard-wood cuttings are usually taken from fall to mid-spring from shoots produced either in the current year (if taken in the fall) or in the previous year (if taken in spring). These cuttings are woody and consequently much thicker.

For most deciduous trees, soft-wood cuttings are the most reliable. A heel cutting is usually more successful than a nodal cutting. A heel cutting should have no more than three nodes. If nodal cuttings are used these should be prepared using a very sharp blade or craft knife as it is very important not to damage the cells of the plant stem by crushing it with a blunt knife or other implement. Nodal cuttings should not be cut with pruning shears as these also crush the stem. Cuttings taken from the lower portion of a tree are usually more reliable. The reason for this is not clear, although it has been observed that cuttings taken at a lower point are stockier and have shorter internodal joints. These cuttings are therefore less sappy and consequently contain more carbohydrate. The store of carbohydrate helps to feed the cutting once it has rooted . Cuttings taken from higher up a tree are usually longer and sappier.

A cutting is prepared by removing the leaves from the lower portion of the cutting. This is then dipped into hormone rooting powder and inserted into the rooting medium. The growing tip should be removed so that the new growth will be produced from the two dormant buds at the top. Retain only half of the leaf area of the two top leaves of cuttings from large-leaved deciduous species, so as to limit water loss. Slight shading of the cuttings is essential to prevent them drying out. A cool greenhouse or a large propagating frame is useful because it provides the humid environment needed for successful propagation.

Bottom heat is also a great asset, though not absolutely essential. Constant spraying of the leaves will boost the success rate because the production of successful cuttings is based on the golden rule of "cool heads and warm feet".

The best season for deciduous soft-wood cuttings is early to mid-summer. Taking cuttings either before or after this period is not impossible, but the success rate will be much lower. Mid-summer cuttings are best because the period of daylight is longest at this time of the year.

There is no ideal rooting medium for the taking of successful cuttings. Some gardeners manage to achieve a very high success rate by using either pure peat or pure sand or a mixture of equal parts of peat and sand. The peat should be medium to coarse grade sphagnum moss peat and the sand should be as sharp as possible. There are also proprietary brands of grit or gritty material of volcanic origin which are very successful. If in doubt, use a 1:1 mixture of moss peat and sharp sand. An ordinary seed tray can be used, but this is not ideal. Cuttings should be struck in a cutting bed which is at least 3-4 in (7-10 cm) deep. Deep seed trays are perfect for this purpose. Used grow-bags are also very useful. They should have holes punched at the bottom to help drainage, and some sharp sand added to them. As a general rule, fertilizer should never be applied to freshly inserted cuttings or cuttings which have just started to root. Cuttings should not need any fertilizer until they have been growing vigorously for four or five weeks. In the right conditions, freshly inserted cuttings should strike within two to three weeks. So, cuttings taken in early summer should have rooted in plenty of time for potting up in early fall. If only a few cuttings are needed there is no need to use large seed trays: A 5 to 7 in (13 to 18 cm) half-pot is quite adequate. I have these methods satisfactory for most varieties of trees, achieving a success rate of about 90% for trident and ordinary mountain maple (*Acer palmatum*). Varieties of the rarer maples such as Seigen and Chisio are more difficult and here a success rate of 30 to 40% should be considered good.

As a general rule, soft-wood cuttings work well for elms, zelkovas, mountain maples, and trident maples. The easier subjects such as willows, forsythia, and poplar are best propagated from fairly thick hard-wood cuttings. These cuttings could be anything from $\frac{1}{4}$-$\frac{1}{2}$ in (0.5-1.5 cm) in thickness. They should be 9-12 in (23-30 cm) long with or without a heel. They are inserted into the open ground in early or mid-fall, and should start growing in the following spring. They should be left in the ground for a year before they are dug up.

A cold-frame is useful for hard-wood cuttings as it helps to provide a close, humid atmosphere which aids propagation. Soft-wood cuttings can also be used for certain broad-leaved evergreens such as camellias and mahonias.

Evergreen cuttings

The coniferous evergreens that can be propagated from cuttings are all struck from hard-wood material. With the

Far left: Most maples can be propagated from cuttings. These pictures show how trident maple cuttings are made. With a pair of sharp pruning shears, cut off a shoot about 6-8 in long. Make the cut just below the node and remove the top 2 inches of soft growth.

Left: Remove the lower leaves so that only two, three, or four leaves remain at the top of the shoot. Any leaves that are fairly large should be reduced by half so as to reduce transpiration. This usually improves the success rate of cuttings

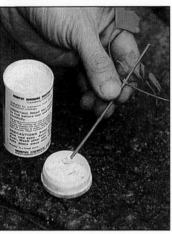

Far left: Dip the end of the prepared cutting into some hormone rooting powder.

Left: After shaking off excess rooting powder, insert the cutting into the rooting medium, which may be either pure peat or a mixture of equal parts of peat and sand. The cuttings should be spaced about 1-2 in apart. Under ideal conditions, most maple cuttings will send out roots within two to four weeks.

exception of the pines, most conifers will root very easily from cuttings. All the junipers (Chinese, needle, and the common juniper), the cypresses (Hinoki and Sawara) and spruces can be propagated in this way. The Japanese black pine (*Pinus thunbergii*) can be struck from cuttings, but the cutting should be dipped in a fairly strong solution of indolebutyric acid and bottom heat is essential. It is very difficult, if not impossible, to strike cuttings of the other pines such as the Japanese five-needle white pine and variants of the Scots pine. However, since they can be propagated quite easily either by grafting (as in the case of the white pine) or from seed, as in the case of some of the Scots pines, it would seem pointless to try to propagate them from cuttings anyway.

Evergreen conifer cuttings can be taken at any time during the growing season, i.e. from the spring right up to the fall. Basically, the same method applies to conifer cuttings as to deciduous cuttings. The rooting medium again could be either pure peat or pure sand or an equal mixture of peat and sand. Always use heel cuttings about 2-3 in (5-8 cm) long, taken from one-year-old wood and about the thickness of a matchstick. Remove the leaves from the lower portion of the stem and dip the stem into hormone rooting powder. Hormone rooting powder helps to improve the strike rate of cuttings, though

Junipers strike very readily from cuttings, ideally about 3 in long. Tear off a young shoot of second year wood which is no thicker than a matchstick.

The best cuttings are those which have a heel. Such cuttings are invariably more successful than ordinary nodal cuttings.

After removing the cutting from the tree it should be inserted quickly into a seed tray filled with pure peat or a mixture of peat and sand.

Cuttings should be spaced 1-2 in apart. These should send roots out in three to four months.

This juniper cutting was taken about a year before the picture was taken. It has certainly produced a lot of root during this time.

Rooted cuttings should be potted on in the spring of the following year into 3- or 5-in pot s.Given the right conditions this cutting should double in size over the next year.

with junipers this is not absolutely necessary. A cold-frame is usually sufficient. If a heated propagator is available this may be used although it is not essential. The cuttings will need to be shaded from the hot summer sunshine if they were taken in the spring or summer. These cuttings will have rooted by mid- to late summer if they were taken early and may be potted up individually in 2 to 3 in (5 to 8 cm) pots later in the year, preferably before the fall. Cuttings taken in fall should be left in their trays to grow for a full year before potting up. Spring cuttings are generally more successful for deciduous and coniferous trees. Cuttings should not be fertilized until they are well rooted and well established. In fact it is probably safer not to fertilize at all until the cuttings have been potted up for two to three weeks. After this a very weak

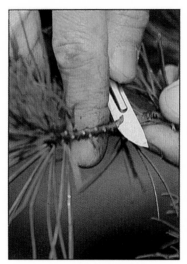

Grafting a five needle pine onto a
Scots pine. Use a one-year-old - to
4-mm thick five needle pine shoot.

The scion for grafting should be
trimmed with a sharp scalpel into a flat
chisel shape.

Below: The grafting is now complete.
This should be kept in a cool
greenhouse for a couple of months
and watered very carefully. making
sure that water does not penetrate
into the newly formed union. Most
white pines which are used for bonsai
are propagated in this manner.

Make a slanting cut in the root-stock to
a depth of about 4 mm and then insert
the scion so that the cambium of the
scion and rootstock match perfectly.

Wedge the scion into the root-stock
firmly and then tie the two together
with raffia or special grafting elastic.
The union may also be painted with
grafting wax to secure the joint.

liquid fertilizer can be applied. A close, humid atmosphere
should be provided for cuttings at all times as this improves the
strike rate considerably. Propagation from cuttings rather than
from seed is still the favorite method for increasing juniper
which is such a favorite bonsai subject.

Crafting

Grafting is usually resorted to by nurserymen for propagating
plant varieties that are not easily propagated by any other way.
In bonsai, the Japanese white pine (*Pinus parviflora*) is a classic
example. It does not grow successfully from seed and those

Air layering by the ring bark method. Make the layering just below the junction of several branches. Cut off redundant branches, leaving three or four above the layering point.

Just below the point at which the roots are desired, cut a ring of bark about 1 in (2.5 cm) long all the way round the branch. This may be done with a scalpel or sharp pruning knife.

Wet some sphagnum moss thoroughly with water or vitamin B1 solution and place it on polythene sheeting about 16 x 12 in(40 x 30 cm).

The moss should now be wrapped around the portion of the trunk where the bark has been removed.

that do grow from seed are rarely vigorous. They are consequently grafted on to the much more vigorous Japanese black pine root-stock. The special maple varieties such as Seigen, Chisio, and Yatsabusa are all grafted on to ordinary *Acer palmatum* root-stock for the same reason.

Grafting is widely used for propagating fruit trees and ornamental trees and shrubs because this is the only way of ensuring the reproduction of particular named varieties of fruit or flower. As a method of propagation, grafting is perhaps the most difficult process for the amateur. With practice however, there is no reason why the amateur should not be as proficient as the professional. The special cultivars of two- and five-needle pines are favorite subjects for grafting in bonsai. European nurserymen have always insisted on grafting two-needle pine scions on two-needle pine root-stock. Similarly five-needle pine scions are recommended for five-needle pine root-stock. In the East however, two-needle pine root-stock is used universally for both two- and five-needle pine scions. Ordinary Scots pine root-stock is very good for most varieties of pines; if Japanese black pine is available for root-stock, so much the better.

The "side cleft graft" is probably the simplest method to use. The best time for grafting is late winter or early spring. Grafting may also be done in late fall, but this is not as good a time as early spring. Choose a Scots pine which has been growing strongly in a pot and which is no thicker than a pencil. Make an incision in the side of the stem fairly near the base. This incision should be $\frac{1}{2}$-$\frac{3}{4}$ in (1.3-2 cm) long. To prepare the scion, use material which has been taken from one-year-old wood and which is about $\frac{1}{8}$-$\frac{1}{4}$ in (0.3-0.6 cm) thick. Trim this piece of material so that it is about 1-2 in (2.5-5 cm) long. Make two slanting cuts, one at a steeper angle than the other, so that the scion ends up looking like a chisel blade. Insert this wedge-

Wrap the polythene round the sphagnum moss ball and tie both ends with string or thin wire. The polythene will retain the moisture.

The completed air layering should be left on the trunk for about a year, until the roots appear

shaped scion into the cleft in the root-stock, making sure that the cambium layers of both root-stock and scion line up exactly with each other. Tie the union of the scion and root-stock very lightly with raffia or the special elastic used for grafting. Never use plastic string or twine to tie the union as this would choke the scion and prevent sap from reaching it. Never let water splash onto the union until it is well established . When watering the plant always water from below. As in the case of cuttings, a humid and close atmosphere aids the success rate. When the union has taken successfully, the scion will grow on and produce more shoots. Do not remove the top portion of the root-stock until the fall. This is best removed in two stages, half of it in the fall and the other half in the following spring.

Air-layering

Air-layering is an old-established method of propagating trees and plants. The Chinese invented this method some 1,500 years ago. It is still commonly referred to as "Chinese air-layering" in horticultural circles.

This is a very satisfying method of propagation for bonsai enthusiasts because fairly thick branches can be propagated in a very short time. Depending on the variety of tree, branches of up to 2 in (5 cm) thick can be successfully air-layered. Branches which have interesting shape and potential as bonsai are ideal subjects for air-layering.

Not all varieties of trees can be air-layered. In my experience all the cypresses, the trident and ordinary mountain maple, zelkova, elm, larch, white pine, black pine, rhododendron, azarea, willow, forsythia, quince, crab apple, cedar,

The bark ring method is not always successful because certain varieties of tree are not able to withstand the very drastic treatment of complete bark removal. A slightly safer method of air layering is the sliver variation of the ring bark method. A tiny sliver of bark is left in order to sustain the upper portion of the branch being layered. This sliver acts as a bridge which continues to supply nutrients from the parent tree to the layering.

The wire tourniquet method is another variation extensively used in bonsai. It is less drastic than the ring bark method and usually perhaps more successful. Select a branch to be air-layered and them take enough copper wire to make a double loop around it.

The double loop is wound around the trunk just below the junction of several branches. The air-layering should produce roots just above the point where the wire tourniquet has been tied.

Using a pair of pliers. tighten the ends of the wire until it bites deeply into the bark. Next, wrap a ball of sphagnum moss around the trunk and tie this up with polythene sheeting. Roots should appear in one or two years.

cryptomeria, cotoneaster, pyracantha, wisteria, hornbeam, and beech can be successfully air-layered.

There are two basic techniques for air-layering—the bark ring and the wire tourniquet methods (see page 38). In the bark ring method, a ring of bark about the same width as the diameter of the branch is removed all the way round. If the trunk is ½ in (1 cm) in diameter, a ring of bark ½ in (1 cm) wide is removed using a sharp knife. However, for thicker branches of say 2 in (5 cm) in diameter, it is advisable to remove only about 1 in (2.5 cm) of bark. For old woody branches of anything over 1 in (2.5 cm) in diameter, it is a good idea to saw the branch from the underside to a depth of about half the thickness of the branch. Dust the portion of branch where the bark has been removed with hormone rooting powder. Wrap a large ball of sphagnum moss around the bare trunk and cover it with a sheet of clear plastic. Bubble plastic is even better since it acts as a good insulator, holding the warmth inside the ball of sphagnum moss. The warmth helps to induce roots more quickly. Tie the plastic sheet at both ends with thin galvanized wire. Water the sphagnum moss occasionally (about once a fortnight). If vitamin B1 liquid is available this will considerably

speed up the rooting process. However, even if vitamin B1 solution is not used, roots can be induced in as little as four weeks in maple, zelkova, elm, and juniper. Other subjects may take a little longer. Pine can take six months to two years to root.

Some trees are unable to withstand the drastic treatment of complete bark removal and the portion which is being air-layered may sometimes die. If this happens, leave a thin sliver of bark in order to sustain that portion of branch: Wisteria benefits from this when using the bark ring method (see page 38). Alternatively, the wire tourniquet method can be used. This is a much slower method, but generally safer. It also has the advantage of swelling the base of the air-layering thus giving it a good potential taper. The wire tourniquet method is particularly suitable for cedars.

For the wire tourniquet method, use fairly thick copper wire ($\frac{1}{8}$ diameter) to wrap around the branch which is to be layered. Tighten the wire with a pair of pliers until the wire bites deeply into the bark (see page 38). Dust the branch with hormone rooting powder and cover the area with sphagnum moss. Cover the moss with bubble plastic and tie the two ends with ordinary galvanized wire. Water occasionally with vitamin B1 solution during the summer. If roots do not appear after the first summer, be patient and leave the ball of moss on for another year or two until the roots do appear. When the roots show through the sphagnum moss (the white roots can be seen quite easily through the plastic sheeting) cut the branch off with a sharp saw or pruning shears. Remove the plastic sheeting very carefully, taking great care not to disturb the sphagnum moss ball. Place the air-layering in a flower pot a bit larger than the root ball and fill up the pot with pure sphagnum moss peat. Do not use a heavy compost (such as John Innes 1 or 2) as the weight of the compost might very easily break the delicate roots. The secret of success lies in using pure sphagnum moss peat. Pure peat is light and also retains heat. This stimulates the initial development of roots more quickly, thereby firmly establishing the tree very early on. In two to three weeks the roots from the air-layering should fill the entire flower pot. When this happens, pot the rooted air-layering on, using a slightly larger flower pot. This will in turn make the tree even more vigorous. Start feeding the potted air-layering after about a fortnight using a weak liquid fertilizer.

Young nursery trees

Nurseries and garden centers are probably one of the richest sources of potential bonsai material for the enthusiast. Most garden centers nowadays have a bewildering choice of shrubs and trees so much that the bonsai enthusiast is spoilt for choice. The increasing use of container-grown material has also made the job of creating bonsai much easier. You can now

Roots have appeared on the layering. Cut the branch off just below the sphagnum moss ball using sharp pruning shears.

Fairly thick branches can be air layered This picture shows a 1 in (2.5 cm) diameter branch which has just been removed from the parent tree.

This branch which has been layered is quite long, well over 35 in (90cm), and has a mass of foliage.

Remove excessive foliage from the layering to reduce transpiration. Some basic pruning can also be done now.

The roots of the layering are clearly visible. Do not remove the moss yet as this may damage the roots.

Pot the layering in pure sphagnum moss peat and water it well. Allow the roots to fill the pot before potting on.

create "instant bonsai" in literally a matter of minutes. The pictures on page 41 will give the reader some idea of the type of material which can be turned into instant bonsai.

When looking for potential bonsai material in a garden center try to look for material which shows obvious promise, For instance, seek out those trees which have interesting trunks. The trunks should also be as thick as possible. Very often in nurseries and garden centers, trees which have crooked trunks are discarded because they will never grow into the straight specimens which ordinary gardeners want. These twisted specimens are ideal for bonsai. Look also for trees which are bushy and have branches growing from fairly low down the trunk. The more branches there are, the greater the scope for creating interesting bonsai shapes. It is also a

An example of typical nursery or garden center material which is suitable for making into bonsai. Shrubs and trees with interesting trunks and branches starting fairly low down are ideal for this. This is a pyracantha bush which is about 24 in (60 cm) high and the same width. probably no more than four or five years old. When the branches have been shaped and pruned it will probably make a nice little bonsai.

This bonsai has been in training for only four years from ordinary nursery stock of *Pinus sylvestris beuvronensis*. It was originally 36 in (90 cm) high but now measures about 24 in (60 cm). The foliage pads are developing well and in a few years the tree should be quite presentable.

Above: This larch is being trained into a 36 in (90 cm) bonsai. It has a trunk

diameter of 3½ in (9 cm). Originally a 4yd (3½ m) tall commercial nursery tree, its top was cut off six months ago and it is well on its way to becoming a fairly handsome bonsai. A new apex has been developed from a side branch and the foliage pads are forming nicely.

Above: This 4 foot (1.2 m) high Japanese maple is being trained into a bonsai from a tree originally 4 yd (3.5 m) tall. It has been in training for only two years. Most of the branches were completely regrown during this time.

Left: This tall zelkova will eventually be made into a bonsai.

good idea when looking at garden center material to prod around the base of the tree because container-grown shrubs and trees are often planted deeper than they need be. Consequently, the base of the trunk could be as much as a couple of inches below the soil level, and the taper will be that much more interesting too.

Nursery stock is probably the most adaptable material for bonsai. Because the trees have already been growing in pots for a long time, disturbing the root ball and reducing it further to fit the bonsai pot will not be as traumatic as digging the tree straight out of the ground. Similarly, the top can be chopped about quite considerably without doing the tree much harm. As a general rule, if about one-third of the root ball is removed then a corresponding proportion of the branches should be removed to maintain a proper balance between root and foliage. Garden center trees are often planted in soil-less compost (i.e. compost which is entirely peat based) whereas compost for bonsai is usually based on a mixture of soil which contains sand and loam in addition to peat. Be careful when

The zelkova shown in the picture on the opposite page was purchased from this nursery. Here, the tree is being lifted from the ground with hydraulic lifting gear. It has, of course, developed much more since it was purchased. In a few years it could be quite unrecognizable as a bonsai.

potting up a garden center tree to make sure that the transition from soil-less compost to soil based compost is not too sudden. After repotting a tree, it is a good idea to keep it in a close environment such as a cool greenhouse. The close atmosphere will aid recovery and help the tree to re-establish itself much more quickly.

Mature commercial trees

Larger specimen trees which are sold for landscaping and other amenity work can offer the bonsai enthusiast a rich source of potential material. These trees are often referred to as "street trees". They are ideal for producing larger specimen bonsai, and the great advantage is that they can be made in a relatively short period of time. The use of large specimen trees for making bonsai is not widely appreciated by the ordinary bonsai hobbyist. However, this practice is common in both China and Japan as it enables the bonsai grower to produce much older looking trees relatively quickly. It is possible to produce a tree with a fairly thick trunk in as little as 15-20 years. Indeed many of the trident maples from Japan which have trunks of 3-4 in (8-10 cm) in diameter are produced in this way. These could easily be passed off as fifty to sixty year-old trees although they are no more than fifteen to twenty years old. The secret of this technique is to grow the trees rapidly in the ground for the first ten to twelve years with occasional undercutting of the roots every other year. Just before it is time to lift it from the ground to make a bonsai, the tree is cut down to the appropriate height leaving only the desired branches in place. A new leader and any new branches which are required will develop over the next few growing seasons.

Meanwhile, the roots should be undercut again to produce even more new fibrous roots over the next few growing seasons. By the end of that time the tree will be ready for lifting

This juniper was collected from the wild just seven months before the photograph was taken. It was found growing in a pocket of gravel high up on a mountainside. Very little shaping has been necessary. It is quite pleasing as it is, with much driftwood and some beautifully shaped branches. It is 20 in (50 cm) high and the trunk is about 2 in (5 cm) in diameter at the base.

and no harm should come to it when it is finally taken out of the ground. This method is extremely attractive to commercial bonsai growers because it saves years of work. As the finer specimen trees become scarcer, this method is bound to become more important.

Basic training and shaping is done from a very early stage. When the seedling is about ⅛-¼ in (0.3-0.6 cm) thick, it is wired into its ultimate shape. While the tree is growing in the ground it is of course fed very heavily. However, it goes without saying that bonsai grown by this method can never look as elegant as those that have been trained from infancy in a bonsai pot.

In mountainous areas such as this, very good bonsai material can be collected. The trees grow naturally stunted in these harsh conditions but the best specimens are often very difficult to remove. However you can sometimes be lucky and find a tree which can be lifted quite easily without much effort.

Collected trees

Although a bonsai is essentially a man-made object, there are trees which are naturally stunted because the conditions in which they grow never allow them to reach their full stature. The harsh cold winds and driving rain at high altitudes, coupled with exposure to ultraviolet light, have a natural

This is fairly typical of the bonsai which are exported in large numbers from Japan. It is a Chinese juniper trained in the informal upright style. This particular tree is 18 in (45 cm) high and about thirty years old. It has a trunk diameter of about 1 in (2.5 cm).

dwarfing effect. Growers of alpine plants will be familiar with these climatic conditions. In high mountains where such conditions exist, naturally stunted pines, junipers, larches, and spruces are commonly found. The Chinese and Japanese have always admired these trees, and in fact they have always regarded them as the best bonsai. There is something special about naturally collected bonsai because they have a freshness which only nature can impart. Art cannot emulate nature in this respect. Harsh environmental conditions leave an indelible imprint on natural collected bonsai.

Professional bonsai hunters in China and Japan used to scour the mountain regions in search of these fine dwarf specimen trees. Many of them risked their lives in the process, but it provided them with a living, and bonsai collectors have had the pleasure of enjoying some very fine trees. Nowadays, natural collected bonsai are becoming increasingly rare because the sources have become exhausted. There are still one or two areas, especially in China, untouched by bonsai hunters, and they may still be a rich source for collected trees. In Japan however there are few areas which have not already been stripped of potential bonsai material.

This larch has been growing in my garden for the past five years. It is now ready for lifting. A circular trench is dug around the tree about 12 in (30 cm) from the trunk. The entire root ball is then lifted onto a piece of plastic sheeting or hessian which is tied carefully so as not to break any of the roots. It can now be moved without risk of damage. Trees collected in this way should be replanted as soon as possible.

In other places beautiful material can be collected, preferably after permission has been obtained from the landowner. Many of my own collected trees are from sheep farms in the mountainous parts of Wales and Scotland. The best places for collecting these naturally stunted trees are on the bleak mountains, where the conditions are harsh. Woods and forests do not often provide good collected material because trees tend to grow straight in forest conditions. Sometimes, though, useful material can be found in areas used as firebreaks, because the trees there are cut down every few years. Trees growing on the outer edges of forests, where much more light is available, can provide a useful source of young seedlings. Again, it should be emphasized that permission must be obtained before any seedlings or young trees are taken.

Trees which are dug up from gardens and hedgerows may also be regarded as collected material because they do not fall into any of the other categories of bonsai sources. Hedges are a very useful source of bonsai because they often contain some very old and gnarled specimens. However, when collecting hedging trees one should ensure that the roots are undercut well in advance before being lifted. If you can avoid it, never try to dig up a tree in one go. It is usually better to prepare the tree for lifting over a period of at least one, or even two growing seasons. The preparation for lifting consists of digging a circular area 1-1½ ft (30-45 cm) away from the trunk and cutting off the main tap and side roots. This will stimulate and promote the development of the fine fibrous roots. When it comes to lifting, the tree will have a system of well-developed fibrous roots to support it. This process will be recognized by those who are familiar with commercial nursery practice as it is referred to as "undercutting" a tree. It is commonly and regularly done to facilitate the lifting of trees for sale. Take the essential tools when you go out on a collecting expedition: a small shovel, a pair of sharp pruning shears and a small pruning saw. With these three basic implements even quite big specimens are manageable. It is also useful to have a supply of plastic sacks, string, and sphagnum moss for wrapping around the root ball when a tree is lifted.

Ready-made bonsai

Perhaps the easiest way to get started in bonsai is to buy a ready-made tree. There are now many fine bonsai nurseries in almost every country, where good bonsai can be purchased. The prices of course vary from place to place depending on how far the trees have had to be transported. A few nurseries are beginning to produce their own native bonsai and these can be very beautiful too. However, there is nothing quite like the genuine article from Asia, because bonsai from the East

When buying ready-made bonsai it is always better to buy a well established tree rather than one which has been potted up only recently. For a novice there is always some risk that the newly potted tree might die through lack of proper after-care. A well established tree should have a mass of healthy roots like this one.

always have a special quality about them. The prices also depend very much on the age and beauty of the tree. A much older tree will naturally cost considerably more than a younger one.

It cannot be emphasized too strongly that bonsai are essentially outdoor plants. They should not be purchased from department stores where they have been kept in a hot and dry environment for weeks on end. Bonsai which have been kept under these conditions will be in very poor condition or very nearly dead by the time they are purchased. If you are buying a bonsai , buy it if possible from an outdoor nursery or garden center, where trees have been growing over a long period in natural conditions. Florists are increasingly selling bonsai and they are probably a much better source than department stores because their atmosphere is usually cool and humid. When buying a bonsai always make sure the tree looks healthy. The foliage should be bright green if it is an evergreen tree. If it is a deciduous tree, then the leaves should look healthy and have the right color for the appropriate time of year; in spring the leaves should be fresh and green, while in fall the trees should have their beautiful seasonal color. Avoid trees which look sickly and which have scorch marks on the leaves. Trees that are badly wired and have deep scar marks should also be avoided if possible as it is quite difficult to get rid of wiring scars.

It is also a good idea to make sure the tree is growing strongly. This can be checked by lifting the tree out of its pot. If growth has been strong and the tree is well established the root mass should come away very neatly from the pot and the white tips of the roots should be clearly visible at the edges. If a tree has been freshly planted in a pot the chances are that it will not be possible to examine the root ball in this way. Consult the nursery staff before doing this. A reputable nursery will sell only trees that are well established and you should have no difficulty getting to see the root ball. As long as the tree is good and healthy there should be nothing to hide.

This *Berberis thunbergii* bonsai has been in training for the last fifteen years. The gnarled old roots were formed naturally by the steady erosion of soil from the earth bank on which it grew for many years; in fact, it was taken originally from a hedge in my front garden. It is 18 in (45 cm) high and approximately thirty five years old. It is planted in the Chinese reclining style with sandstone rocks to complement the tree.

Advantages and disadvantages of the various methods

The different methods of starting bonsai all have their various advantages and disadvantages depending on which species you wish, and are patient enough, to grow.

Starting a bonsai from seed may be a relatively slow process but it is a real pleasure seeing the tree grow from its embryo stage to maturity, and exciting having complete control over its training from the very beginning. Most seedlings are usually more vigorous than their counterparts which have been growing from cuttings. There is also the chance of discovering a "sport" or hybrid when trees are grown from seed.

Cuttings reproduce exactly the characteristics of the parent tree. They are relatively easy to make and in situations where seed is unobtainable, may be the only viable method of propagation. Trees grown from cuttings do not always produce roots uniformly distributed around the trunk. Furthermore, trees grown from cuttings do not usually develop a good taper at the base.

Grafting is resorted to when most of the other methods are not viable. This is a relatively quick way of producing a fairly mature tree. Grafting also has applications for styling where special cosmetic effects are required to improve the looks of a mature bonsai. If a tree lacks branches in the appropriate places, new ones can be grafted on fairly easily.

Air-layering is a particularly convenient means of creating a good looking bonsai from a mature branch of a bigger tree. It is a very rapid process and often saves years of work. It is also a cheap way of creating a mature bonsai.

Nursery trees and mature commercial trees are a convenient means of creating large bonsai relatively quickly. This method is inexpensive and similar in some respects to collecting from the wild.

Collected trees from the wild provide the most beautiful bonsai. However, one has to look hard for the best specimens. Collecting trips can of course be great fun too, but it is absolutely essential that permission is obtained before trees are lifted.

Buying a ready-made bonsai is obviously the simplest way to begin a collection. A proper bonsai looks attractive right from the start. The owner can use that tree as a model for others which are being trained. It is a good idea to have a mix of finished bonsai and trees which are in the process of being trained. Having nothing but young seedlings that bear no resemblance to bonsai can be disheartening because of the years of waiting to see the finished product. Most bonsai enthusiasts have trees produced by all the various methods which have been described above. Experimenting with the different techniques in order to gain confidence and knowledge is all part of the fun and enjoyment of bonsai.

Group planting of seven European larch. The oldest tree
here is about thirty years old and measures 30 in (80 cm) high.
The arrangement is planted in a large oval tray. Larches
are extremely versatile and make excellent individual
specimens; they can also be adapted for use in groups.
Larches are perhaps most spectacular in the fall
when their leaves are a brilliant golden-yellow color.

CHAPTER 4

SUITABLE TREES

Most trees and shrubs can be made into bonsai . A bonsai is after all only a tree in a pot—albeit an aesthetically designed one. However, it would be grossly misleading to suggest that any and every tree is suitable for making into a bonsai ; some are, others are not.

The suitability of a tree for bonsai depends on two broad groups of factors: the horticultural and the aesthetic.

Among the horticultural factors are considerations such as whether a tree could stand up to hard and frequent branch and root pruning, and whether the tree could tolerate being confined in a small pot over an extended period of time. The pliability of the branches is also an important consideration . The aesthetic factors include considerations such as the plant's growth habit, the length of the internodal joints, the size of the leaf in relation to the size of the tree, the texture of the trunk and bark surface, the fineness of the twigs and branches, and the color and shape of the leaves.

Most trees can stand up to frequent branch and root pruning provided it is done judiciously. The horticultural factors are not normally the ones which cause the bonsai artist the greatest problems; aesthetic considerations are more often than not the ones which determine the choice of a particular variety of tree for bonsai work.

The list which follows is only a guide to the more popular varieties of trees which are used for bonsai. It should not be regarded as comprehensive, based as it is solely on my personal experience of growing bonsai. There are no doubt many other varieties of trees and shrubs which can be adapted for bonsai very easily. This holds true for all geographical regions, the tropical and the temperate.

The following varieties of coniferous trees are suitable for bonsai.

Cedar *(Cedrus* spp.*)*

There are three species in this genus which are highly suitable for bonsai. They are:

C. *atlantica* (Atlantic cedar)

C. *deodara* (Deodar cedar)

C. *libani* (cedar of Lebanon)

All cedars like full sun and good drainage. Extra grit should be added to the standard bonsai compost mixture (one-third peat, one-third loam and one-third grit or sharp sand) . They do not like to be overwatered. In fact they are one of the few conifers (junipers and pines are the others) which stand up to drought well. They appreciate some winter protection. Do not repot them too often as their roots break very easily. Once every three years for ten- to thirty-year-old trees is quite adequate. Cedars air-layer quite easily using the wire tourniquet method.

Cryptomeria (*Cryptomeria* spp.)

The cryptomeria is sometimes referred to as the Japanese cedar or sugi. There is only one species in this genus—*Cryptomeria japonica*. The varieties suitable for bonsai are:
C. *japonica* "Elegans"
C. *japonica* "Bandaisugi"
C. *japonica* "Jindaisugi"
C. *japonica* "Elegans" has loose feathery foliage. It is green in summer and turns bronze in winter. This tree needs to be pinched hard in order to get tight growth. The other two cryptomerias are dwarf forms which have been developed over the years. Both are very slow growing and have very compact foliage pads bright green in color. "Jindaisugi" is the faster growing of the two. All cryptomerias need a lot of water. They appreciate some shade in summer and should be protected in winter. The growing tips should always be pinched with thumb and forefinger; scissors should not be used on the foliage as they will cause brown marks where it has been cut. Cryptomerias prefer a loamy soil and the bonsai compost should therefore be modified so that the loam content is 50%. All cryptomerias layer easily. They also strike very easily from cuttings.

False cypress (*Chamaecyparis* spp.)

There are only two species in this genus which are really suitable for bonsai. They are the Hinoki cypress and Sawara cypress. The other species in this genus are quite difficult to make into good bonsai because the branches and leaves do not lend themselves to this type of work.

Ch. obtusa (Hinoki cypress) varieties particularly suitable for bonsai are "Nana", "Nana Gracilis" and "Kosteri". The whorls of leaves on the Hinoki cypress are very attractive and they are the distinguishing feature of this tree. The leaves have a good deep green color. The texture of the foliage and the bark also make it interesting.

Ch. pisifera (Sawara cypress) . The varieties particularly suitable in this species are *Ch. pisifera* "Boulevard" which has fine feathery foliage and Ch. pisifera "Squarrosa" which has soft a feathery blue-gray foliage. The older leaves of both the Hinoki cypress and Sawara cypress tend to die back in the fall. The dead leaves should be removed from the tree as they look ugly. It is usually quite difficult to encourage new leaves to sprout from older wood. These cypresses layer easily and can be grown from cuttings fairly easily too. They prefer partial shade in the summer and do not like too much water. The standard compost may be used, although they prefer slightly more loam in the mix.

I made this Atlantic cedar into a bonsai only seven years ago. It is just over 20 in high and is grown in the slanting style. It was developed from ordinary garden center material.

Fir *(Abies* spp.*)*

This genus does not provide many varieties suitable for bonsai . Only the Korean fir (*A. koreana*) and the Japanese fir (*A. firma*) really lend themselves to bonsai work, otherwise the branches are either too stiff or the needles too long.

Ginkgo *(Ginkgo biloba)*

This is a unique tree, a relative of the conifers with an ancient lineage. It is often referred to as the maidenhair tree. Ginkgos are usually grown in the clump style. They like full sun and plenty of water. They appreciate winter protection. Cuttings should be taken in late summer or early fall using semi-hard-wood. They layer easily by any of the three standard methods. The seeds also germinate easily. For good fall color, use low nitrogen fertilizer from mid-summer onwards. Trimming of branches should be left until mid-spring. They prefer free-draining loamy soil.

Hemlock *(Tsuga* spp.*)*

There are two species which are suitable for bonsai, T. canadensis and *T. sieboldii*. The leaves of both can be reduced in size by root restriction . They do not like too much water and need repotting roughly once every three years. Use the standard bonsai compost

This small Hinoki cypress bonsai was developed from a cutting eight years ago. It is a delightful little tree and has already appeared at several of the annual Chelsea Flower Shows held in London.

Left, and *above* This ancient ginkgo is estimated to be about ninety years old. It is grown in the traditional clump style and is 30 in (80 cm) high. The leaves are extremely pretty both in shape and color. The picture above shows the trunk in great detail.

Juniper *(juniperus* spp.*)*

The junipers provide a rich and varied source for bonsai. Indeed some of the finest and most elegant bonsai come from this genus of extremely hardy and long-lived trees. In Japan the really fine specimens of bonsai junipers are invariably a couple of centuries old or more. Their twisted trunks lend themselves to the driftwood style. Most junipers like full sun and only a modest amount of water. However, they can stand wet conditions provided drainage is good. The natural habitat of junipers is heathland, scrub country, and desert. They are therefore extremely drought-resistant trees. When grown as bonsai, junipers benefit from regular feeding. The dead driftwood areas should be treated regularly with lime sulfur in the spring and summer. The standard bonsai mix can be used but some extra grit should be added to it. Some Japanese growers recommend a 1:1 mix of loam and sand for junipers. Watch for scale insects and red spider; the former insects can be particularly harmful to junipers. When pests appear they should be sprayed immediately.

All junipers layer easily and can be grown from cuttings quite readily. They can also be raised from seed *J. communis* and *J. rigida* grow easily from seed. Pruning should be done in spring, but pinching is necessary throughout the year. To improve the color of the leaves before a show, feed with a nitrogenous liquid fertilizer and keep the tree in partial shade. The list of junipers suitable for bonsai is a long one, but the following varieties are perhaps the most popular.

J. chinensis "Sargentii" (the Chinese juniper). There still seems to be some confusion over the classification of this particular juniper. In Britain it is often sold as *J. media "Shimpaku"*.

J. chinensis "Kaizuka" (also known as Hollywood juniper)

J. chinensis "San Jose"

J. conferta (also called the shore juniper)

J. chinensis "Blaauw" (this is very similar to "Shimpaku")

J. chinensis "Globosa Cinerea"

J. chinensis "Hetzii"

J. chinensis "Pfitzeriana"

J. communis is a wild form commonly found in Europe and Central Asia.

The cultivar *J. communis* "Hornibrookii" is very suitable for bonsai.

J. procumbens

J. rigida is the best of all the "needle junipers" for bonsai. There are many forms of rigida. Some have short needles, others have slightly longer ones. The driftwood on rigida is without doubt the most spectacular of all the junipers.

J. squamata "Meyeri" is very good for tall bonsai and for tall groups. It benefits from hard and regular pinching to encourage new growth from old wood.

J. virginiana can be used but does not make good specimens.

Larch (*Larix* spp.)

For some unknown reason, larch is not often used for bonsai in Japan but it is certainly good bonsai material. Larches are very hardy and can stand up to pruning well. Although they are deciduous, they have the double advantage of looking like pines when in leaf, and also go through the seasonal color changes which range from apple green in the spring to rich golden yellow in the fall. They also have the ability to put out new shoots from very old wood - most other conifers do not. If a branch is needed in a particular spot, a little patience is all that is required . They like full sun in spring and early summer but partial shade during mid-summer. They do not require winter protection. Standard compost is adequate. Pinching of the new shoots in early summer will result in two crops of leaves and branches in a year. All the varieties of larch are suitable for bonsai. *L. L eptolepis* (Japanese larch) is best for bonsai. The branches are much finer than those of the other larches. The tips of the European larch (*L. decidua*) are gray-brown whereas the tips of the Japanese larch are a slight bronze color. This is a slightly stiffer tree than the Japanese larch. *L. x eurolepis* (Dunkeld larch) has very attractive cones which are produced on trees as young as ten years.

Dawn Redwood *(Metasequoia glyptostroboides)*

This tree was discovered as recently as 1945 in China. It is sometimes referred to as the "Fossil Tree", because it was thought to have been extinct. It makes attractive bonsai although the branches tend to spring upwards. Growing requirements are similar to those of the larches.

Pine *(Pinus* spp.)

Along with the junipers, pines are probably the most important conifers for bonsai. They are ideal both from the horticultural and aesthetic standpoints. Most pines are grown from seed and quite nice trees can be produced in as little as eight or nine years by this method. The Japanese white pine (*P. parviflora*) can also be grown from seed but more vigorous trees are produced by grafting on to Japanese black pine root stock. Similarly, the sports of Scots pine have to be grafted on to ordinary Scots pine root-stock in order to retain the characteristics of the particular cultivar. All pines love full sun but only a modest amount of water. Black pines in particular like to be kept fairly dry. Pines love sandy soil and older specimens prefer an even more gritty compost (as much as 60% sand, and the rest made up of loam and peat in equal

This Chinese juniper, which was imported from Japan in the mid 1960s, was featured in the 20th Century Fox film *The Final Conflict* starring Rossano Brazzi and has been seen by millions of people throughout the world. It is grown in the informal upright style and measures 75 cm high. Although the precise age is not known, it is probably well over 70 years old.

Common juniper collected from the wild. It is 40 cm high and probably about 50 years old. It has had virtually no training. The driftwood areas were not created artificially, but naturally by exposure to the harsh elements.

This Japanese white pine (*Pinus parviflora* "Himekomatsu") has been grafted on to Japanese Black pine rootstock, hence the gnarled old trunk. It is trained in the informal upright style and is 24 in (60 cm) high. Although pines such as this are exported from Japan in large numbers, many countries have banned the import of pines and junipers from abroad for fear of introducing diseases into their own forests.

A group of five Ezo spruce, the tallest of which is 30 in (75 cm). These trees have been growing together in this group for the past twenty-five years. I find it a prolific source of cuttings.

proportions). For younger pines, the standard bonsai mix may be used. Young pines can be fed very heavily throughout the summer to produce rapid growth. Constant pinching of the young candles in early summer will induce new shoots to break further back from old wood. This helps to create good looking foliage pads. All pines can be air-layered, but the Japanese black pine and Japanese white pine are particularly suitable for propagation by this method.

As a rule, pines do not need to be repotted as frequently as other trees. Young trees (i.e. under five years) need repotting every year, trees between five and fifty years old every other year, trees between fifteen and fifty, once every three years, and trees over fifty years old once every four years. The very old trees (i.e. over hundred years) need to be repotted even less frequently, once every five or six years. The best time to repot is in mid spring and the best time to wire pines is in the fall.

Heavy branch pruning is best done in the fall. The cuts should be sealed with grafting wax in order to stop bleeding. The following varieties of pine are suitable for bonsai.

P. cembroides (Mexican nut pine)

P. contorta (beach pine)

P. densiflora (Japanese red pine). This is not a very vigorous tree and not many Red pines are seen as bonsai these days. "Tanyosho" is the variety most often used for bonsai.

P. griffithii (Bhutan pine) . This makes quite a graceful bonsai.

The long needles are reduced in size by root restriction.

P. mugo (mountain pine). Most varieties of mountain pine make nice bonsai.

P. nigra (European black pine). Good for literati.

P. parviflora (Japanese white pine). There are probably a couple of hundred cultivars of this species, most of which were either discovered or developed in Japan. These short-needled or "Yatsubusa" varieties are especially popular today. "Himekomatsu" is currently one of the favorite White pines for bonsai.

P. strobus (Weymouth pine). The variety "Nana" can be developed into nice bonsai. Their biggest drawback however is that they tend to bleed very heavily when pruned. Never prune in the spring as bleeding will be profuse. The best time to prune is late fall.

P. sylvestris (Scots pine) . Beautiful bonsai are being created with this native British species. They are particularly suitable for literati bonsai. The variety *P. sylvestris* "Beuvronensis", which is a very bushy plant, makes beautiful formal and informal upright trees. When well grown, it is almost indistinguishable from the Japanese white pine, although hardier and more reliable in Europe. The other Scots pine cultivars such as "Watereri", "Westonbirt", and "Frensham" all make very good bonsai.

P. thunbergii (Japanese black pine) makes majestic trees. It is easy to grow from seed. Cuttings are also possible, but strong hormone rooting powder or solution is needed. Cuttings are usually deployed for the variety "Nishi ki" or "Cork Bark Pine".

P. virginiana (sc:rub pine). This pine will grow in almost any soil and can make quite pleasing bonsai.

Yew podocarp *(Podocarpus macrophyllus)*

The Chinese are very fond of using Podocarpus for bonsai. They are similar in many respects to the yews in their growth habit. They like full sun and some winter protection.

Californian Redwood *(Sequoia sempervirens)*

This species makes very impressive bonsai especially if grown in the formal upright style. The trees put out new branches quite readily from old wood and need treating in the same way as cedars (see page 52).

Wellingtonia *(Sequoiadendron giganteum)*

They make fine formal upright and informal upright bonsai. Treatment as above.

Spruce *(Picea* spp.)

The spruces are more suitable for bonsai than the firs. Varieties which make good bonsai are:

P. Asianis gracilis
P. abies "Nidiformis"
P. abies "Pygmea"
P. glauca "Echiniformis"
P. glauca "Albertiana Conica"
   P. glehnii (Sakhalin spruce) is sometimes wrongly referred to as *P. jezoensis* or ezo spruce. This is by far the most commonly used spruce for bonsai. It has very fine leaves and a delicate habit. It is particularly useful in group plantings and for trees grown on rocks. Spruces do not like too much water. They are very similar to the pines in their soil requirement, i.e. they like sandy compost. They also love full sun throughout the year.

Swamp cypress *(Taxodium distichum)*

Like the willow, the swamp cypress needs plenty of water and full sun during the growing season. In fact the tree and pot should be immersed in a basin of water throughout the summer. The compost should be loamy, i.e. 50% loam and 25% each of peat and sand. In Florida particularly, bonsai enthusiasts have used this species to create some really fine specimens.

Yew *(Taxus* spp.)

Yews are difficult to train into good bonsai but, when trained they make handsome trees. The two varieties most often used are:
Taxus baccata (English yew)
Taxus cuspidata (Japanese yew)
   They prefer a loamy soil and may be placed either in full sun or semi-shade.

■

The following varieties of broad-leaved trees are commonly used for bonsai:

Alder *(Alnus* spp.)

Alders are vigorous trees but, when grown as bonsai, their internodal joints and leaves can be considerably reduced in size. Alders generally grow beside streams and lakes and they

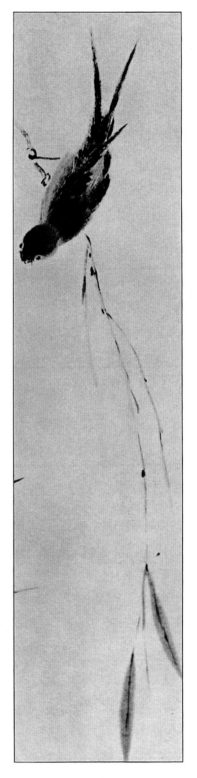

love wet conditions. During the summer, alders should be placed permanently in water. They like loamy soil (60% loam, 20% peat, 20% sand) and full sun. They can be leaf-pruned every year. Varieties suitable for bonsai are:

A. glutinosa
A. nitida
A. cordata

Ash *(Fraxinus* spp.*)*

All species of ash tend to be vigorous trees especially when soil conditions are favorable. However, in harsh environmental conditions, ash can acquire beautiful gnarled trunks. Except for the weeping form, most varieties of ash are suitable for bonsai. They like loamy soil, full sun and lots of water. Leaf cutting can reduce the size of leaf quite considerably. Repotting should be done every other year.

F. excelsior and *F. ornus* are very good varieties for bonsai.

Bamboo *(Arundinaria* spp.*)*

Most of the dwarf forms of ornamental bamboo are suitable for accent plantings. Some of the taller varieties are used for groups.

Beech *(Fagus* spp.*)*

Beech make extremely handsome bonsai. Like most deciduous bonsai, they are admired more during the winter than the summer. The common beech (*F. sylvatica*) tends to keep its brown leaves throughout the winter and this can be extremely attractive when most other deciduous trees have lost their leaves. The Japanese beech (*F. crenata*) has beautiful white bark and this is highly admired in winter when the rest of the tree is bare. Beech grow on chalky soil and the bonsai compost should try to reflect these conditions. The trees prefer a loamy soil (50% loam) and lots of water. Semi-shade during the summer is necessary to prevent the leaves from being scorched. They are otherwise fairly hardy.

Below: The colorful fruit of *Berberis thunbergii.* This is a detail of my tree which is shown on page 48. Berberis make extremely attractive bonsai, as they flower and very regularly.

Left: An old collected beech trained in the split trunk style, probably at least fifty years old but collected only two years before this picture was taken. It is 25 in (65 cm) high and has a 6 in (15 cm) diameter trunk. The original tree had been cut back regularly over the years in a forest plantation as part of a fire-break. Material of this kind makes ideal bonsai.

Berberis *(Berberis* spp.*)*

This is a shrub rather than a tree but it still makes a good bonsai. The spring and fall coloring is quite spectacular. Berberis thunbergii is particularly good for bonsai. Berberis is often grown as a hedging plant and beautiful old specimens can be

obtained from this source. They will grow in almost any soil. Water moderately and keep in full sun. Full sun will induce good fall color.

Birch *(Betula* spp.*)*

Most of the birches can be used for bonsai either as single trees or in groups. B. pendula and B. nigra are good for this use. However, the branches tend to die back and trimming and pruning should therefore be left until early spring. The wood is also susceptible to fungus diseases. Birches prefer slightly acid sandy loam, and lots of water and semi-shade during the summer.

Box *(Buxus* spp.*)*

Boxes are highly suitable for bonsai because of their small leaves. The Chinese are particularly fond of box for bonsai. They are very hardy trees and can withstand drought well. They grow in almost any soil and require only moderate watering. They prefer semi-shade conditions.

B. sempervirens and most of its cultivars, including the variegated ones, work very well. They air-layer easily and grow from cuttings readily too. Box make extremely attractive *mame*.

Horse chestnut *(Aesculus* spp.*)*

Horse chestnuts are not normally favored for bonsai because of their large leaves. However, with root restriction and leaf cutting the leaves can be reduced quite considerably in size. A. *hippocastanum* responds well to this treatment and can make very impressive trees given time. *A. parviflora* is also suitable for bonsai. Horse chestnuts grow in almost any soil and prefer semi-shade in summer.

Dogwood *(Comus spp.)*

Dogwoods are often overlooked for bonsai, but quite nice specimens can be produced with a little patience. The common dogwood (*C. sanguinea*) and cornelian cherry (*C. mas*) are very suitable varieties. They are not fussy trees, and the standard compost will do.

Elm *(Ulmus* spp.*)*

Not many species in this genus are suitable for bonsai because their leaves are usually too large. However, the Chinese elm (*U.*

parvifolia) is one of the favorite deciduous subjects for bonsai. It has small leaves (about ½ in [1.25 cm]) long) and some recent cultivars have leaves which are no more than ¼ in (0.5 cm) long. It produces a fine tracery of branches if constantly pinched. A variety of English elm which is suitable for making into bonsai is the Plot elm (*U. plotii*) named after a certain Dr. Plot. When grown as a bonsai the Plot elm is almost indistinguishable from the Chinese elm. Elms prefer loamy soil (50% loam, 25% peat, 25% sand) and lots of water. Elms are quite hardy and do not generally require winter protection unless temperatures fall below 25°F (–4°C).

Hazel *(Corylus* spp.)

Hazels are not often used for bonsai but the pollarded stumps of the common hazel (*C. avellana*) can make quite interesting trees. Root restriction and leaf pruning will reduce the size of the leaf quite considerably. Like most broad-leaved trees, they prefer loamy soil. Water moderately during the summer and keep in a semi-shaded position. They should not be repotted too often as the leaves will not reduce in size.

Holly *(Ilex* spp.)

A number of species in this genus can be used for bonsai. The holly used for Christmas decoration (*I. aquifolium*) does not make good single trunk bonsai. It can however be grown in the clump style. *I. serrata* which has much smaller leaves is more successful. Hollies love plenty of leaf mold in the soil and the standard mix should therefore have a handful of leaf mold added to it. They prefer semi-shade conditions and moderate amounts of water. *I. crenata* also makes a good bonsai and is usually grown for its berries.

Hornbeam *(Carpinus* spp.)

Hornbeams are extremely vigorous trees renowned for their hard timber. However, they can make fine bonsai. Almost all the species in this large genus are suitable for bonsai. The more common species of hornbeam are:
C. betulus (or common hornbeam)
C. cordata
C. caroliniana
C. laxiflora (red-leaf hornbeam)
C. japonica (Japanese hornbeam)
C. turczanino (a small leaf form)
C. tschonoskii

Above: Detail of the hornbeam below showing the extremely powerful-looking root structure. The roots should be the center of attraction when this bonsai is ready for showing.

Right: This hornbeam (*Carpinus betulus*) is being developed into a bonsai from hedging material. It is a fairly large tree with a main trunk about 22in (55 cm) high and 3 ¹/₂ in (9 cm) in diameter. It has an exquisite exposed root structure and would therefore make an extremely attractive bonsai in the exposed root style. All the branches on this tree have regrown over the last two years. The apex is being developed from the current year's growth. Constant pinching of the shoots should produce dense foliage pads in a very short time. Trees in training can be grown in large wooden boxes like the one shown. They facilitate training because they can be moved around as desired.

Hornbeams prefer a rich loamy soil (50% loam to which cow manure has been added, 25% leaf mold, 25% sand or grit). They love plenty of water and semi-shade in the summer. As they are such vigorous trees yearly repotting is necessary. They need to be pruned in the early spring. They propagate easily from both hard- and soft-wood cuttings, air-layerings and seed. Hornbeams are extremely adaptable for bonsai because they produce new branches and shoots so readily.

Ivy (*Hedera* spp.)

Although a creeper, ivy can be made into very attractive bonsai. Wild ivies are commonly found creeping up the trunks

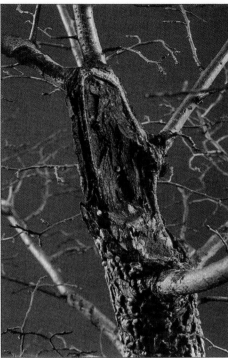

Above: Plot elm (*Ulmus plotii*) being trained as a formal upright bonsai. This tree has had only four years' training. It is 26 in (65 cm) high and has a trunk diameter of 2 $\frac{1}{2}$ 6 cm). Note the overall triangular shape and the fine tracery of branches achieved by constant pinching of the new shoots each summer. This bonsai has been developed from a commercial nursery tree originally 3 yd (3m) tall.

Above center: A detail of the elm on the left showing where the trunk was cut in order to develop the new leader. It is already healing well and in a few years time the callus should have healed up completely.

of large trees. If they are dug up very carefully with sufficient root, quite good bonsai can be created from ivy using the already well established creeping trunk. They are very hardy and drought resistant and grow in almost any soil either in full sun or semi-shade.

Above: Ivy bonsai developed from a root which once girdled the trunk of a sycamore tree in my garden. This bonsai is 20 in (50 cm) high and is being trained in the exposed root style.

Lime *(Tilia* spp.)

The small leaf varieties of lime are suitable for bonsai. These are
T. x europea
T. cordata

Although fairly vigorous trees, limes should be repotted only every second year as root restriction will help the leaves to grow small. Reduction in leaf size can also be achieved by leaf cutting. Limes can be grown in standard bonsai compost. They appreciate lots of water in summer and can be placed in full sun. They propagate very easily from cuttings and from seeds.

Maple *(Acer* spp.)

The maples are by far the most important genus for deciduous bonsai. Not only are their spring and fall colors spectacular, but their growth habit can be very interesting too. The tracery of their branches in winter can be quite magnificent. Some bonsai enthusiasts consider the Japanese maple to be at its most beautiful in winter because the

branches are so delicate and graceful. Unfortunately, maples grow naturally only in the northern temperate zone and cannot therefore be grown in warm climates. Although maples are normally associated with the Japanese maples (*A. palmatum* and *A. japonicum*) many of the other species make fine bonsai too. The following species may be used for bonsai.

A. campestre (field maple)

A. capillipes (snake bark maple)

A. circinatum (vine leaf maple)

A. ginnala (Amur maple)

A. griseum (paper bark maple)

A. platanoides (Norway maple)

A. pseudoplatanus (sycamore)

A. rubrum (red maple)

All of these will grow in almost any soil and the standard bonsai mix may be used. As many of them are vigorous trees they should not be repotted too often. Once every other year will suffice. They should be defoliated in the summer to induce smaller leaves and watered copiously and placed in full sun.

Japanese maples
(*Acer palmatum* and *A. japonicum*)

The Japanese maples deserve a separate mention because they are so important to bonsai. A. palmatum is a slightly more vigorous tree than A. japonicum. The two species are easily confused and the way to distinguish them is by the leaf shape and texture. A. palmatum usually has five to seven deeply incised lobes and the leaf itself is smooth in texture. A. japonicum on the other hand has seven to eleven less deeply incised lobes (i.e. less than half the length of the leaf). The leaves are also slightly downy in texture when they unfold. Japanese maples prefer slightly acid soil and the standard bonsai compost is quite adequate. They like plenty of water, but do not like the full sun in mid-summer. In early spring and fall they may be placed in the full sun when it is not so hot. On hot sunny days maples need to be watered at least twice a day. Aphid and scale insects are particularly troublesome pests. Keep a careful watch from early summer through to fall against insect pests on the underside of the leaves as they may cause bad disfiguration. During the growing season the young growing tips need to be constantly pinched. Leaf cutting may be practised on large-leaved varieties, but it is important to ensure that the plant itself is strong and vigorous. Never leaf-cut a sickly tree. Leaf-cutting usually produces smaller leaves which will also have a better fall color. Maples should be repotted in early spring. Branch pruning is better done in winter when the sap is not rising in the tree. If pruning is done too late, the tree bleeds profusely. Branches should be wired just before the new leaves emerge. Young trees up to ten years old should be repotted every year, while older trees up to fifty years old, should be repotted every other year. Much older trees should be repotted once every three years.

Maples should be fertilized from late spring right up to early fall. For good fall tints a low-nitrogen fertilizer should be applied from mid-summer onwards. Maples air-layer very readily. They are also very easy to grow from seed. The rarer varieties of Japanese maples are usually grafted on to A. palmatum root stock. Japanese maples may be grown from cuttings also. The cuttings should be soft-wood cuttings taken early in June. *A. palmatum* is much easier to propagate than *A. japonicum*.

Both Japanese maples appreciate winter protection.

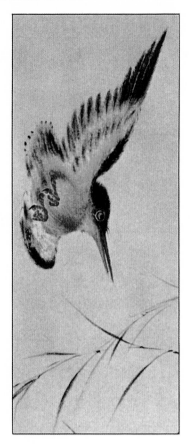

Trident maple *(A. buergerianum)*

The trident maple is an extremely vigorous tree. When grown in the open ground it can produce long 3 to 4 ft (90 to 120 cm) shoots in one year. If grown in the open ground the trunk could be ¾ in (2 cm) thick after five years. A fifteen-year-old tree could acquire a trunk diameter of 3-4 in (8-10 cm) if grown in the ground. Trident maples should be trained from fairly early on. The basic shape is made when the tree is no more than ⅛ in (0.3 cm) thick. Trident maples are used extensively for root-over-rock style bonsai. They are such vigorous trees that the roots develop very rapidly and can become quite pleasing in a relatively short space of time. Tridents grow in almost any type of soil but a good compost for trident bonsai is 50% loam, 25% grit, 25% leaf mold. Being so vigorous, they need to be repotted every year. They can be fertilized quite heavily with high-nitrogen fertilizer in early summer. From mid-summer to early fall they should be fed with a low-nitrogen fertilizer for good fall color. They need to be constantly pinched throughout the growing season. Tridents layer very easily and can be propagated from both soft- and hard-wood cuttings. They grow easily from seed too. Tridents like a lot of water during the growing season but they need to be protected from the direct sun in the mid-summer. Tridents are slightly tender and should therefore be given protection from early winter onwards.

Oak *(Quercus spp.)*

Oaks are not often used for bonsai but they do make nice specimens. Oak collected from the wild can be very beautiful. In Europe the common oak (Q. robur) makes good bonsai and with root restriction the leaves do become quite small. The European holm oak (Q. ilex) is another popular tree for bonsai.

Above: Detail of the maple on the right showing the gnarled old trunk. The tree is so old that much of the wood has decayed. It has to be treated regularly with a bitumen-based wood preservative in order to stop further rotting.

Right: This magnificent Japanese mountain maple is 40 in (100 cm) high and 42 in (105 cm) wide with an 8 in (20 cm) diameter trunk. It has been grow n in the broom-cum- formal upright style. It is estimated to be well over one hundred years old and was imported from Japan in mid-1960s.

Page 71, top left: Japanese mountain maple grown in the informal, upright style. The tree is 28 in (70 cm) high and has very dense fine branches. This bonsai breaks many of the conventional design rules, but despite this is still very attractive. As is often the case, it is by breaking the rules that new percept ion and insight are achieved.

Page 71, top right: This twenty-year-old trident maple has a 4 $\frac{3}{4}$ in (12 cm) diameter trunk. It is 36 in (90 cm) high and was imported from Japan five years ago. All the branches have regrown during the past three years. The tree is being reshaped with a view to eliminating the ugly apex. It has a very nice radial root spread and an interesting curved trunk. The white marker indicates the front of the tree.

Page 71, below left: An extremely handsome specimen of *Sageretia theezans* trained in the split trunk style, 30 in (75 cm) high and 18 in (45 cm) wide. It was imported from western China in 1979 and is reputed to be over one hundred years old. It is planted in an antique Chinese stoneware pot. The center of attraction or focal point is undoubtedly the hollow trunk. The design is typically Chinese in character.

Page 71, below right: Common oak (Quercus robuij can be trained into very attractive bonsai. They are extremely hardy trees, able to withstand drought and very severe winter conditions. They are also very long lived. This particular bonsai has been t rained for seven years in the informal upright style, and is 25 in (65 cm) high.

Oaks like a loamy soil and the compost should therefore be 50% loam, 25% peat, 25% grit. Oaks propagate very easily from seed and can make very rapid growth if grown in the open ground. Bonsai oaks should be repotted every other year.

Sageretia theezans

This tree is used extensively in China for bonsai. It is known in China as the bird plum. It has tiny pink flowers and is evergreen in milder climates. In the temperate zone it tends to be deciduous. As it is slightly tender it needs winter protection. In my experience, sageretias have survived temperatures as low as 27°F (−3°C). They propagate easily from hard- and soft-wood cuttings. They prefer a loamy soil: 50-60% loam, and peat and sand in equal proportions.

Southern beech *(Nothofagus* spp.)

Southern beech make quite attractive bonsai. *N. antarctica* is particularly good as an individual specimen tree, while N. procera is suitable for making into groups. They grow in well-drained loamy soil. The standard bonsai mixture is adequate.

Spirea

This is really a shrub and it is particularly useful for *mame* and accent plantings.

Stewartia monadelpha

The stewartias are used quite extensively in Japan for making into groups. They are similar in many respects to the southern and the ordinary beeches.

Sweet gum *(Liquidambar styraciflua)*

Liquidambar are usually grown for their spectacular fall colors. They make good bonsai and resemble the Amur maple in many ways. They grow in almost any type of soil, and the standard bonsai mixture is suitable. They should be watered moderately and like full sun.

Vitex *(Vitex sp.)*

V. chinensis or the chaste tree is usually grown as a shrub but the stump is used extensively in China for creating gnarled old bonsai. The tree has aromatic leaves and pretty mauve flowers. It grows in loamy soil and the bonsai compost should therefore have about 60% loam, 20% leaf mold, and 20% sand. They propagate very easily from soft-wood cuttings. They like full sun in summer and should be given winter protection. They should not be pruned too hard if flowers are desired.

Willow *(Salix spp.)*

A number of species in this genus are suitable for bonsai. The weeping willow (*S. babylonica*) makes a nice weeping tree while S. caprea (goat willow) can be trained into any style. They are particularly spectacular when derived from gnarled old trunks collected in the wild. All willows love rich loamy soil and the compost should therefore consist of 60% loam, 20% leaf mold, and 20% sand. Willows should be stood in water throughout the summer and never allowed to dry out. They like full sun and some winter protection.

Zelkova *(Zelkova spp.)*

This is a small genus which resembles the elm in many respects. The zelkova used for bonsai is Keyaki (*z. serrata*). It is sometimes referred to as the Japanese gray-bark elm. They are extremely vigorous trees, perhaps even more so than the trident maple, and for this reason should always be trained in a container from as early as possible or else they grow rampant. This is the favorite species for broom-style bonsai. Very often some young seedlings will show a natural tendency toward this style. These can then be trained in containers.

Zelkovas are not fussy about soil. The standard bonsai compost will suffice. They need moderate amounts of water and may be kept in the full sun during spring, early summer and fall. They should however be kept in semi-shade in mid-summer. They need winter protection. Zelkovas are best propagated from seed, although air-layerings of fairly thick branches—up to 2 in (5 cm) diameter—can be produced in a fairly short space of time.

General care of fruiting and flowering trees

Most fruiting and flowering trees prefer a rich loamy soil with added well-rotted farmyard manure. They love full sun and plenty of water during the summer. They should be fed with high-nitrogen fertilizer during the early summer, but from mid-summer onwards their diet should be changed to a high-potash, low-nitrogen fertilizer.

Pruning and repotting are best done immediately after flowering, except in the case of wisteria which should be repotted in early spring before the flowers open. A compost made up of 50% loam, 25% peat or leaf mold, and 25% sharp sand would suit most flowering trees.

TREES GROWN FOR FRUIT AND FLOWER

Almond (Prunus dulcis)

The almond is a very pretty tree. It flowers very early, sometimes in late winter. Almonds love chalky loam and the compost should therefore have 50% loam, 20% leaf mold, 30% sand to which some lime has been added. They like full sun and adequate watering during summer. Like most fruiting and flowering trees, almond bonsai are usually grafted.

Apricot (Prunus mume)

This is similar in many respects to the almond. They like full sun and lots of water during the summer.

This beautiful Satsuki azalea was imported from Japan twenty years ago. Although it flowers regularly, its flowers tend to be too large for the scale of the tree. Despite this, the flowers are still the main attraction.

Azalea (*Rhododendron* spp.)

There are two azaleas which are extensively used for bonsai: the Satsuki (*R. lateritium*) and the Kurume (*R. obtusum*). Both are quite stunning when in flower. Older specimens also make very handsome bonsai when not in flower because of their massive trunks and beautifully arranged branches. Azaleas are peat-loving plants and the compost must therefore be predominantly peat-based. A good formula is 50% peat, 20% manure or leaf mold, and 30% sharp sand. They like full sun except in mid-summer. They appreciate a feed of iron chelates in early spring. The best time to prune is after flowering, but hard pruning should be done only every second year for the best flowering results. Azaleas respond well to hard pruning and are very obliging in producing new shoots quite readily from old wood. They can be propagated easily from cuttings or air-layerings. The best cuttings are those from the current year's wood but which have hardened sufficiently at the base. Mid-summer is the best time for taking cuttings, although spring and fall cuttings can also be quite successful. A great deal could be written about azalea bonsai, but in a general book of this nature only the fundamentals can be covered.

Camellia (*Camelfia* spp.)

Camellias do not make good bonsai as a rule because the scale of the leaves and flowers is not in keeping with the rest of the tree. However, the Chinese and Japanese are fond of using C. japonica and C. reticulata for bonsai. Camellias naturally grow in acidic conditions and the compost used for azaleas would therefore work equally well for them. They like semi-shade conditions during summer.

Southern beech (*Nothofagus antarctica*) trained as a bonsai. I developed this tree four years ago from ordinary nursery material and planted it in a stoneware pot I made myself.

This crab apple was grown from seed collected from Kew Gardens in London twelve years ago. It is now 20 in (50 cm) high and trained in the informal upright style. It has flowered regularly for the last three years.

Pea tree *(Caragana* spp.)

C. aborescens makes a nice weeping tree. The flowers, which are creamy white or pink, resemble those of wisteria. They like full sun and rich loam.

Celastrus orbiculatus

This is a climbing plant which can be trained into a nice looking tree. It is grown for its very beautiful seed pods.

Cherry *(Prunus spp.)*

All the cherries love alkaline soil. The compost should therefore be about 50% loam, 25% leaf mold, and 25% sand. They are fairly hardy trees. They love full sun and adequate water in the summer.

Of the many species of cherry, those particularly suitable for bonsai are:

P. avium (or gean)

P. padus (bird cherry)

P.lusitanica (Portugese laurel)

The Japanese cherries however are the ones which have the most beautiful flowers and they, fortunately, can be successfully dwarfed too. Most of the varieties are suitable for bonsai. These are:

P. sargentii (all its various forms)

P. serrulata (all its various forms)

P. subhirtella (winter flowering cherry)

Cotoneaster Spp.

This is a large genus comprising shrubs and small trees. Most of the varieties are suitable for bonsai. *C. horizontalis* is perhaps the most popular variety for bonsai. Other varieties suitable for bonsai are:

C. frachettii

C. microphyllus

C. dammeri

C. simonsii

They grow in almost any soil and the standard bonsai compost will suffice. They like full sun and moderate amounts of water. They do not require winter protection.

Crab apple *(Malus spp.)*

Crab apples grow well in the temperate zone. They are very hardy as bonsai and they flower and fruit consistently. Crab apples like well-drained loamy compost and the standard fruiting bonsai mix will do. They can be potted either in late fall or early spring and they like full sun and plenty of water during the summer. Crab apples are particularly prone to attack by pests such as woolly aphis, greenfly, blackfly, and borers. Spray the tree the moment you notice any signs of infestation. It is important also to continue spraying throughout the winter to kill any larvae and insects that may be harbored in the trunk or soil.

The followi ng varieties of crab apple are suitable for bonsai.

M. baccata

M. cerasifera

M. floribunda

M. halliana

M. hupehensis

M. sargentii

M. sieboldii

Crape myrtle *(Lagerstroemia indica)*

This is really a tropical tree and should be kept indoors in winter. However, from late spring to early fall they can be grown outdoors. They like lots of water and plenty of sunshine. They prefer a rich loamy soil with 60% loam, 20% leaf mold, and 20% sharp sand.

Golden bell tree *(Forsythia* spp.*)*

Forsythia are extremely hardy shrubs and they will grow in almost any kind of soil. They love full sun and adequate water in summer. The stumps of old trees can be made into very interesting looking bonsai. They can be trained into almost any desired shape, but this needs to be done from a fairly early stage.

Grape *(Vitis* spp.*)*

Grapevines may seem rather an odd choice but they can be made into nice bonsai. The old stumps from vineyards are particularly useful in this connection. Vitis "Brandt", which has small-sized fruit and beautiful fall leaves, makes a very attractive bonsai.

Hawthorn *(Crataegus* spp.*)*

Hawthorns grow in almost any soil but they prefer rich loam. The standard bonsai mix may be used or a mix containing 50% loam, 25% leaf mold, 25% sand. They are extremely hardy trees.
   Varieties suitable for bonsai are:
C. crus-galli (cockspurthorn)
C. monogyna (may tree or common hawthorn)
C. oxyacantha (similar to C. monogyna but with more rounded leaves)
C. laevigata (most varieties including "Paul's Scarlet")

Jasmine *(jasminum* spp.*)*

The winter flowering jasmine (J. nudiflorum) makes very good bonsai. The stumps of climbers make old-looking trees. The standard flowering bonsai compost is suitable. They are fairly hardy trees. They like plenty of sunshine during summer to induce good flowering buds.

Judas tree *(Cercis siliquastrum)*

Grown mostly for its beautiful mauve-pink flowers which emerge directly from old wood. They are not particular about soil. The standard flowering bonsai compost is suitable.

Laburnum *(Laburnum spp.)*

Laburnum are not often seen as bonsai but they make very pretty flowering trees. They grow in almost any soil but prefer loam. They love full sun and adequate water in summer. Slugs love laburnum leaves and should therefore be kept well away from them during the growing season .
L. vulgare and *L. alpina* are particularly suitable for bonsai because of thei r small racemes of flowers.

Lespedeza *(Lespedeza* spp.)

The Chinese are quite fond of lespedeza for bonsai. Both *L. bicolor* and *L. thunbergii* are suitable; they grow easily from seed and are quite vigorous shrubs. They need to be constantly nipped back during the summer. They love full sun and plenty of water.

Lilac *(Syringa* spp.)

Lilac is not ideal for bonsai but old stumps can be used.
S. vulgaris (common lilac) and its various cultivars are suitable for bonsai.
S. x *persica* (dwarf lilac) makes very nice small bonsai. The scented flowers are delightful in spring. All lilacs prefer chalky loam, full sun, and moderate amounts of water.

Magnolia

Magnolias are grown for their lovely flowers. However, only those with small flowers are suitable for bonsai. They include :
M. kobus
M. liliiflora
M. stellata
Magnolias prefer an acid soil. The compost should therefore consist of 40% peat or leaf mold, 30% loam, and 30% sharp sand. They like full sun and they need to be repotted every year immediately after flowering.

Peach (Prunus persica)

Peach bonsai require the same treatment as the Japanese flowering cherry.

Pear (Pyrus spp.)

Most varieties of pear can be grown as bonsai . They love rich loam, full sun, and adequate water. They prefer to be repotted in late fall rather than after flowering in spring.

Pomegranate (Punica spp.)

Pomegranates are not grown just for their beautiful fruit and flower, but also for their exquisite trunks. Pomegranates are native to western Asia and the Mediterranean region and are therefore slightly tender in cooler temperate zones. They need good winter protection. The two commonest varieties used for bonsai are P. granatum and *P. granatum* nana. They propagate very easily from seed, layering, and cuttings. Cuttings of very large plants strike fairly readily when inserted in sharp sand Pomegranates prefer a fairly acid, but rich, loamy soil. The bonsai compost should consist of 40% loam, 30% leaf mold or manure, and 30% sand. They love full sun and only moderate amounts of water. Pomegranates do not stand up to pruning

Young seedlings can be made into extremely attractive group plantings. These three small cotoneasters planted together in a shallow tray look quite spectacular in their fall foliage. Although the trees are only six years old they flower and fruit regularly. The composition is 10 in (25 cm) high. The red berries will stay on the trees throughout the winter as long as birds do not strip them.

well and often die back for no apparent reason . Although pomegranates are native neither to China nor Japan they have become, over the past 1,000 years, one of the favorite plants in Asian folklore. Most of the named cultivars which exist today were originally developed in China and Japan.

Cinquefoil *(Potentilla* spp.*)*

This shrub makes quite a nice bonsai. Potentillas stand up to pruning well and are very hardy shrubs. They grow in almost any soil and prefer full sun in summer and moderate amounts of water.

Quince *(Chaenomeles* spp. *and Cydonia* spp.*)*

Chaenomeles or flowering quince is often confused with cydonia or the true quince. The two genera are however quite distinct. *Chaenomeles* are grown primarily for their beautiful flowers, while *Cydonia* are grown for their fruit. *Chaenomeles japonica* has small orange flowers and small apple-shaped fruit. Chaenomeles speciosa is a much bulkier shrub and has larger prettier flowers which range from white to pink and red. Their fruit are also slightly larger.

The two species of Cydonia which are grown for bonsai are *Cy. oblonga* and *Cy. sinensis*. The fruit in both species are very distinctive. Many people, however, regard the fruit as being too large for the tree. Quinces will grow in almost any type of soil, although they prefer rich sandy loam. The standard flowering bonsai compost will suffice. They propagate easily from seed, hard- and soft-wood cuttings, and air-layerings. They also graft well. They should be repotted in early spring either before or after flowering. Pruning should be done in late summer when one or two buds of the current season's wood are retained as these are the ones that provide next year's flowers. Quinces love full sun and only moderate amounts of water. Wiring needs to be carefully done as the branches tend to be brittle.

Spindle tree *(Euonymus* spp.*)*

The spindle tree is grown mainly for its lovely fall color and for its very unusual seed pods. They prefer a chalky soil and the standard fruiting bonsai compost will suffice. The two most popular varieties for bonsai are :
E. alatus
E. europaeus
They like full sun and moderate amounts of water.

Serissa sp.

This is a favorite bonsai subject with the Chinese. It has no special requirements except some winter protection.

Viburnum *(Viburnum* spp.*)*

The viburnums can make quite impressive bonsai. They are particularly handsome if grown in the mUltiple trunk style. V. plicatum tomentosum and V. tinus are most suitable and grow well in almost any type of soil. The standard fruiting bonsai mix will suffice. They like full sun and modest amounts of water.

Wisteria *(Wisteria* spp.*)*

A wisteria bonsai in bloom is a memorable sight because the flowers can be quite stunning. A well-trained specimen can bear forty to fifty racemes of highly scented flowers. The varieties of wisteria suitable for bonsai are:

W. floribunda (Japanese wisteria)

W. frutescens

W. sinensis (Chinese wisteria)

The named varieties are usually grafted, but wisteria also air-layer very easily and can be grown from seed. However, trees which are grown from seed take much longer to flower and are therefore not recommended for growing as bonsai. Wisteria can be grown in full sun during the summer provided they are given a plentiful supply of water. They need some winter protection. Like most flowering trees, wisteria prefer a well-drained loamy soil, with plenty of manure added to it. The standard flowering compost will be suitable.

Importing bonsai

From time to time, bonsai enthusiasts may get the opportunity to import trees from abroad. However, every country has a system of plant health regulations designed to prevent the introduction or spread of plant pests and diseases. It is important that all rules and regulations are strictly observed.

The need for such a system was recognized at the turn of the twentieth century, but it was only after the First World War that a common system of plant health certification or phytosanitary certification was agreed upon by the international community. Under the arrangement every country may exercise its right to restrict the importation of certain plants which could introduce or spread pests and diseases.

Over the years bonsai growers have chosen to classify
trees by their various distinctive styles. The split trunk
style shown here is just one of them.

CHAPTER 5

BONSAI
STYLES

To a layman, a bonsai is a bonsai; they all tend to look very much alike. But to the expert, no two Bonsai are ever identical. They all have their distinguishing features which make them unique. Just as no two human beings are absolutely identical—so with bonsai, no two trees can ever be exactly the same.

Through the centuries, bonsai practitioners have found it convenient to classify bonsai into broad divisions based on their appearance. These groupings have come to be known as the classical styles. So, trees which have a straight perpendicular trunk are called formal upright trees. Those which have sinuous S-shaped trunks are called informal upright trees, and so on. There are about thirty separate recognizable styles in bonsai, and the ones listed in this book represent only the major ones.

The Chinese and Japanese are very fond of classifying although the various styles were developed long before names were given to them. The bonsai artists first created the designs and the observers later grouped them together into identifiable categories for ease of reference.

Bonsai styles were devised essentially for the convenience of enthusiasts. The followers of bonsai probably found it convenient to refer to the various bonsai styles rather than describe each one of them in detail. I prefer to group all the various styles into three broad generic classes. This classification is based on the number of trunks or trees in the bonsai composition. These categories are

1 Single trunk styles
2 Multiple trunk styles
3 Multiple tree or group styles

The three broad categories can be subdivided into their more detailed classifications.

Single trunk styles

i) Formal upright *(Chokkan)*
ii) Informal upright *(Moyogi)*
iii) Slanting *(Shakan)*
iv) Windswept *(Fukinagashi)*
v) Splittrunk *(Sabamiki)*
vi) Driftwood *(Sharimiki)*
vii) Broom *(Hokidachi)*
viii) Cascade *(Kengai)*
ix) Semi-Cascade *(Han kengai)*
x) Weeping *(Shidare-Zukuri)*
xi) Literati *(Bunjin)*
xii) Exposed root *(Negari)*
xiii) Root-over-rock *(Sekjoju)*
xiv) Planted on rock *(Ishi seki)*

Multiple trunk styles

i) Twin trunk *(Sokan)*
ii) Tripletrunk *(Sankan)*
iii) Multiple trunk *(Kabudachi)*
iv) Root connected *(Netsunagari)*

Multiple tree or group styles

i) Group planting *(Yose ue)*
ii) Planted on rock
iii) Landscape *(sai-kei or pen-jing)*

The fact that there are so many styles in existence today does not mean that they are all popular. As in all aesthetic matters, style is very much subject to the whims of taste and fashion. The cascade style is a good example of how tastes have changed . A century ago the cascade style was very popular. Now it is no longer fashionable, largely because cascade trees are very difficult to transport. A few decades ago the contorted and tortuous styles which the Chinese tended to favor were all the rage: today, however, with the boom in interest in things natural, a more sympathetic style has developed. Trees are meant to look like real trees and not like grotesque animals.

An analysis of the bonsai styles seen at major Japanese exhibitions in the 1980s revealed that about 25% of all trees displayed were in the informal upright style, 12% in the multiple trunk style, 12% in the formal upright style, a further 12% were in the group style; about 10% were in the twin trunk style, another 10% were in the split trunk and driftwood styles, about 7% in the root-over-rock style, 4% in the slanting style, 4% in the semi-cascade style and about 4% in the landscape and classic cascade style. The same data when analyzed another way reveal that about 60% of all the trees displayed were bonsai with a single trunk, about 25% with several trunks and the rest were in group plantings and tray landscapes.

SINGLE TRUNK STYLES

Formal upright style

In this style, the trunk of the tree is absolutely straight, rising vertically out of the ground from a radial root system. The trunk should taper very gradually from the base all the way up the tree.

Trees which grow in this fashion are majestic specimens often to be seen in the grounds of stately homes, or in the middle of large open fields where they grow unhindered and without having to compete with other trees for food and light

Although the formal upright style might appear simple and easy to emulate, it is in fact one of the most difficult styles to realize. Attention to detail is all-important and any little carelessness soon shows up as a major fault.

The arrangement of branches for most bonsai styles is basically the same. The cardinal principle to bear in mind is that the front of the tree should always be uncluttered. The front should be more open than the rear, where there should be more branches to provide the foliage density needed to create the illusion of depth and perspective. The lowermost branch of the tree should start from about one-third of the way up from the base. All the subsequent branches should be positioned evenly around the trunk. The overall shape of the tree should as far as possible, be conical.

The secondary branches and twigs on each of the main branches should resemble the shape of a spear head. The disposition of the branches should be such that they do not overhang each other, otherwise the lower ones will be deprived of light and eventually wither and die. Sunlight is, of course, absolutely essential for the health of any tree. Without sufficient light, the photosynthetic process cannot proceed and the leaves will not be able to produce the food needed to sustain the tree as a whole.

Informal upright style

The informal upright style is perhaps the most popular of bonsai styles. This is because it is much easier to find trees which are not growing absolutely straight. Most trees have natural kinks or twists in their trunk and are therefore more easily adapted to the informal upright style. The style is typically characterized by the lazy S-shape. Because the trunk design of a typical informal upright tree is based on the shape of an "S", the positioning of the branches is not quite so straightforward as is the case in the formal upright tree. The branches must emerge from the trunk at precisely the right positions, namely the outside of the bends or elbows or else the design will not be satisfactory. They should never start from inside a bend. As in the case of the formal upright design, the overall shape of an informal upright tree should be basically conical.

Slanting style

This style is so called because the general slope of the trunk is highly pronounced, certainly more so than in the informal upright style. Whereas in the informal upright style the trunk leans only slightly (i.e. between 10° and 20° from the vertical) in the slanting style the slope is about 45° from the vertical. In fact

Opposite: Semi-cascade Japanese hornbeam. The apex is 12 in (30 cm) above soil level and the tree is 35 in (90 cm) wide. This bonsai is so old that much of the original trunk has rotted away. However. this only adds to the beauty and character of the specimen.

Opposite: Collected larch grown in the windswept style. This is one of my favorite collected trees. 25 in (65 cm) high and 30 in (75 cm) wide. The tree was about fifty years old w hen collected; the top was already dead and only one major side branch was alive. I jinned the two little branches on the right to emphasize the windswept effect and planted it in a modern stoneware pot I made to complement the very powerful-looking trunk. After this photograph was taken the two lower subsidiary branches on the left were also jinned.

the slope in the slanting style is so pronounced that it is very aptly known by this name.,

While the general direction of trunk slope is in one direction, it is quite in order for the trunk to meander slightly to the right and the left as it rises from the base of the pot to the apex.

The surface roots of a slanting style' tree are probably more important than those in any other style of bonsai . This is because a slanting tree has an inherently unstable appearance. However, the feeling of instability can be largely mitigated if the surface roots look convincing enough to give the impression that the tree is well anchored to the soil and therefore incapable of being toppled over.

The slanting style is really an amalgam of the formal upright style and the informal upright style. If the tree itself has a straight trunk that leans heavily to one side, then the branch arrangement rules of the formal upright style could be applied directly.

The slanting style is suitable for both deciduous and evergreen trees. However, conifers are on the whole slightly better suited to this style of bonsai. Branches should be arranged to lie horizontally or droop slightly downwards, but not upright since this would not be in keeping with the general character of the style.

Windswept style

In this style of bonsai the artist seeks to reproduce the visual effect of a tree which is constantly being blown by the wind. Such trees are a common sight along the coast. They invariably lean away from the sea because the direction of the prevailing winds is landwards.

The trunk and the branches of a windswept tree lean in one direction only and are often bleached white by the harsh salt-laden winds. Because it somehow always manages to survive by bending with the wind, a windswept tree is a symbol of fortitude and tenacity in the face of great adversity. Indeed, this theme is a familiar one in bonsai because bonsai artists through the ages have been inspired by the sight of trees which mirror the indomitable spirit of man.

Jin and driftwood highlights on a windswept bonsai always work well because windswept trees in the wild have precisely these features.

Split trunk style

This again is a style which is copied directly from nature. As a tree ages, the trunk usually decays giving rise to some very interesting shapes and patterns. Hollow trunk trees are

commonly seen in ancient forests and they are favorite hiding places of small mammals, birds, and even children. Hollow or split trunks are a sign of old age and bonsai which have split trunks invariably convey the same impression of antiquity. Split trunk bonsai do not follow any precise design rules. The arrangement and disposition of branches are usually informal or natural. A trunk which has been hollowed out needs to be carefully watched as rotting can very quickly set in. If this happens, the rot can spread to the other parts of the tree.

Deciduous species of split trunk trees should be hollowed out at frequent intervals and painted with a tar-based tree preservative paint. The best time to do this is in the middle of summer when the tree is most likely to be dry. In winter the trunk is invariably wet and preservative should not really be painted on damp wood. For evergreen conifer species, a split trunk tree looks more elegant if painted with lime sulfur. This not only preserves the dead wood, but also makes it aesthetically pleasing.

Driftwood style

In the driftwood style large sections of the trunk and certain branches are deliberately made to look like bleached driftwood. This effect may be created either artificially by stripping the bark and cambium from a live tree, or it can be created from a tree that is already partly dead. The dead portion can be carved using sharp carving tools, and later whitened with lime sulfur to give the impression of natural aging by the sun , wind, and rain . It is a very dramatic style and the layman is usually intrigued by the fact that a tree is able to survive at all with so little of it still alive. This style is highly demanding aesthetically. The area of driftwood is usually the center of interest and the entire design of the tree should be carefully built around this feature. Because so much of the tree is just dead wood, great care must be taken to ensure that the tree survives. Preservation of the dead wood is achieved by frequent application of lime sulfur during the summer. This is probably the best way of ensuring that the wood does not rot. If wet or dry rot sets in, it must be carved out to prevent it spreading.

Broom style

Like most of the other classical bonsai styles, the broom style is one which is often seen in nature. The trunk is absolutely straight and the branches are arranged in the shape of an inverted, fan-shaped broom . Because the main attraction here is the fine tracery of branches, the broom style is invariably created from deciduous trees. The zelkova and Chinese elm

are the favorite subjects because they produce very delicate branches and twigs which can be appreciated in winter when the trees have lost all their leaves. Zelkovas in particular lend themselves to this style of bonsai because the seedlings display a natural tendency to develop multiple forked branches from a very early age.

Broom-style bonsai can also be created from fairly thick-trunked trees by simply cutting the tree at the appropriate place, carving out the top with a chisel, and letting the branches grow again like a pollarded tree. In three to five years a fairly pleasing broom style tree can be produced by this method. Broom-style trees look best planted in fairly shallow oval or rectangular pots.

Above: Trunk detail of a one-hundred-and-fifty-year-old Chinese juniper bonsai. The trunk is 4 in (10 cm) in diameter and only a fifth of it is still alive. The driftwood is preserved by treatment with lime sulfur twice a year.

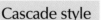

Cascade style

The cascade style is an ancient Chinese design which derives its inspiration from trees growing out of cliff faces and rock crevices. Chinese artists were very fond of painting such trees because they evoked in them a deep sense of admiration. After all, who could fail to be impressed by the sight of a little tree struggling to survive by clinging tenaciously to a rock face high up in the mountains?

The creation of an attractive cascade bonsai is an exacting task. To begin with, most trees have a natural tendency to grow upwards, whereas in a cascade, growth has to be encouraged in the opposite direction. A cascade tree cannot be created by merely bending a pencil-thick seedling over the edge of a tall pot, for such a tree could never really pass as a cascade bonsai. A good cascade should preferably have a short conical head but it must have a fairly thick trunk that curves downwards as close as possible to the point where it rises from the pot. The subtle curves of a cascade demand real sensitivity, and the creation of a beautiful specimen is most satisfying. The cascade is similar to the literati style in having an impressionistic effect with a certain magical quality about it.

Semi-cascade style

The semi-cascade style is a variant of the full cascade style. Broadly speaking, any bonsai with a horizontal or near-horizontal trunk would qualify as a semi-cascade tree. Some bonsai purists would classify all cascade trees that do not extend beyond the base of the pot as semi-cascade specimens. However, this cannot be regarded as a rule since the Chinese, for instance, use very tall pots for their classic cascade trees.

These pots are often 2-3 ft (60-90 cm) high, and the ends of the cascade trees do not fall below the base of the pot. The Chinese sometimes refer to the semi-cascade style as the

Above: Detail of Japanese mountain maple showing the trunk and branch structure. Notice the gradual taper of both the trunk and branches. This tree has probably been grow n from a seed or cutting and trained in a pot for most of its life. It has never been "chopped".

"looking over the water" style since trees which exhibit this characteristic are often found on the edges of rivers and lakes. The position and form of these trees often give the impression of a person peering over the water's edge. The semi-cascade style is full of poise and elegance.

Above: This elm is being trained in the broom style. It is 32 in (80 cm) high and has a trunk diameter of 3 in (8 cm.) It was purchased three years ago from a tree nursery as a 8 ft (2.5 m) standard. The tree was chopped right down to about 12 in (30 cm) and all the branches have been developed since then. In another few years it should become quite a nice-looking bonsai.

Weeping style

The weeping style is reserved for trees that have branches that weep naturally. Trees such as the weeping willow, weeping cherry, weeping peach, tamarisk, and Caragana arborescens are ideally suited to this type of bonsai because their full-size counterparts exhibit precisely the same habit.

The weeping style of bonsai is very Asian in character, and is a common theme in popular Chinese paintings. Indeed, the willow pattern, which was such a favorite theme among the nineteenth-century pottery manufacturers, is based on the weeping style. At the turn of the twentieth-century, this

91

style of bonsai was very fashionable, the common varieties used were the weeping peach bonsai grafted with both red and white flowers. These trees were usually planted in highly colored, deep, round pots. Weeping peach bonsai are not as popular today, and with the exception of the weeping willow, few weeping trees are now shown at bonsai exhibitions.

The weeping style is essentially a hybrid style. The main trunk is usually based on any of the basic single trunk styles (such as the formal upright style, the informal upright style, the semi-cascade style, etc.), and the weeping branches are merely superimposed on the basic trunk design. Consequently, weeping trees do not necessarily have to be planted in deep pots. The pots which are suitable for the basic trunk styles are also suitable for trees which have weeping branches. Weeping trees look equally elegant in both deep and shallow pots ,depending on the basic trunk design. Weeping deciduous trees lend themselves to this style of bonsai.

Literati style

Of all the bonsai styles, the literati style is without doubt the most sophisticated both in terms of concept and visual design. This is understandable when one bears in mind the origins of the literati style. The literati style is so called because it is based on the paintings of trees created by the "Literati".

The literati were scholars and artists of the highest standing, the elite of Chinese society. Their paintings were usually of landscapes with trees and plants depicted growing in the natural (mountain) settings. Pines and junipers were the favorite tree subjects, largely because there were so many of them sprouting out of inaccessible mountain cliffs and crags, the favorite haunts of these scholarly men.

The trees painted by the literati are, strictly speaking, impressionist paintings because they are images of trees perceived in the artist's mind. And yet they are in a sense very real too because trees with these unusual shapes are occasionally found growing wild in the high mountains.

They owe their distinctive shapes to constant exposure to harsh climatic conditions. Trees with "natural" literati shapes can be found in alpine and arid regions throughout the world.

The trunk, with its subtle twists and bends, is the primary area of interest in literati-style bonsai. These may appear unnatural but they are neither grotesque nor ugly, but on the contrary rather beautiful.

The design emphasis of literati bonsai is so heavily focused on the trunk that only a minimum of foliage should be retained to give the impression of a live tree—excessive foliage would be distracting. Similarly, the pot for literati bonsai must be as unobtrusive as possible so that the viewer's attention remains directed almost entirely at the trunk. It is for this reason that evergreens such as pines and junipers (and sometimes

deciduous conifers such as larch) are the favorite subjects for literati.

The newcomer to bonsai may not immediately appreciate the aesthetic beauty of the literati style, but it is difficult to resist for long. The literati style of bonsai is becoming increasingly popular in the West because of its timeless charm .

Exposed root style

This is a rather grotesque style of bonsai and (not surprisingly) it is not often encountered today. The roots are deliberately grown above the soil surface and this can be achieved in a number of ways. The easiest method is to encourage a tree to grow deep into an open and friable soil mixture. The main roots can be trained as if over an invisible piece of rock. Repeated pruning of the ends of the main roots to be exposed will eventually stimulate the growth of fibrous roots at the point of cutting. The entire root system should be lifted from time to time so that it can be examined to ensure that it is developing in the desired manner. When the main roots have thickened adequately, the entire root system can be lifted for potting up. The main roots to be exposed should be allowed to grow above the soil surface, leaving only the fine fibrous roots anchored in the pot.

The exposed root style of bonsai is somewhat reminiscent of trees growing in the brackish mangrove swamps of the tropics. The knee roots of mangrove trees rise well above the soil and water level, and look rather like the elongated limbs of some weird prehistoric animal.

Another less grotesque variant of the exposed root style is that in which the roots grow tightly matted together to form one solid mass. The matted roots will, in due course, coalesce to give the appearance of a gnarled old trunk.

Root-over-rock style

Rocks have always been an integral part of bonsai tradition. This is because the Chinese incorporated rocks into their garden and bonsai design from early times. The Chinese, from emperor to peasant, have occasionally become obsessed with rocks. Indeed there was a period of "petromania" in Chinese history. Aesthetically shaped rocks, symbolizing the craggy mountains so admired by Chinese artists, were placed in gardens with bonsai and so assumed a new realism. Suddenly these miniature landscapes seemed to come alive.

The rocks that are used today with bonsai are still intended to symbolize mountains and mountain scenery, although they are less dramatic than they used to be.

Above: A collection of literati bonsai I created from six-year-old Scots pines grown from seed. Young seedling pine are ideal for this style; indeed their slender trunks are not much use for anything else. Needle junipers and larches also make extremely handsome literati bonsai.

Opposite: Weeping willows are ideal for training into weeping style bonsai. This particular tree is fifteen years old and was grown from a cutting. The height of the main trunk is 16 in (40 cm). It is planted in an antique Chinese pot and displayed on an antique Chinese stand. The weeping branches have to be cut right back to the main trunk every three or four years as they tend to become too thick. Willows should be made to stand in water throughout the summer, or drying-out will cause the leaves to shrivel.

Right: Collected common juniper with jinned trunk grown in the semi-cascade style. Like most collected junipers which already have exquisite shapes and do not require much further refinement, this tree has had virtually no training. The driftwood here has formed naturally.

In the root-over-rock style of bonsai the rock is now simply an appendage of the tree. The tree, rather than the rock, has become the focus of attention. This may well be the correct approach from the point of view of bonsai, but the loss of a certain charm and romanticism is sad. Trees grown in root-over-rock style are usually admired most for their beautiful roots.

The root-over-rock style is technically very difficult to achieve. It can take many years for the roots to clasp a piece of rock tightly before it can be considered a good root-over-rock bonsai. This type of bonsai is usually started by draping the roots of a young tree over a piece of rock. The roots are then tied over the rock with plastic string or metal wire. Tree and rock are planted together in deep rich soil and the tree roots encouraged to grow downwards. The tree is left to grow in the ground for five to six years completely undisturbed. The roots and rock may be inspected every other year, but the tree itself should not be lifted.

When it is time to lift the tree, some of the top branches should be reduced so that the tree does not become unstable. If on inspection, the roots appear to have clasped the rock well, the whole tree, including the main roots, should be severed and lifted out of the ground. The tree may now be planted either in a deep training box for another couple of years so that the upper branches can be trained in the desired shape.

A good root-over-rock bonsai can take anything from four to ten years to create. The more vigorous species are the most common subjects as the whole process is less time consuming. Trident maples are therefore a good choice for root-over-rock. White pines are sometimes grown in this style, but take much longer. In theory of course, any tree can be trained in the root-over-rock style. It is merely a question of patience.

If a very beautiful piece of rock is used in conjunction with a root-over-rock tree, the composition as whole must be very carefully designed and balanced. The exquisite and eye-catching features of the rock must not be obscured by draping roots, nor, by the same token, must the rock itself be so dramatic that the beauty of the tree is diminished. Ideally, the tree and the rock must form a unified whole.

Planted on rock style

This style of bonsai is more in keeping with the original Chinese concept of miniature landscapes in which rocks denote mountains and the bonsai represent the real trees in miniature. There is no deliberate attempt here to drape roots over a rock. The tree is merely planted in or on a rock so that it resembles a real tree growing in a natural setting.

The tree should be planted in a suitable crevice without obscuring the rock's interesting features. Both young and old

A fine example of the root-over-rock style. This trident maple, an example of an extremely popular subject for this type of bonsai, was imported from Japan in the mid 1960s. It is 18 in (45 cm) high and about sixty years old.

trees may be used and the aim is to create a unified composition. In this style of bonsai, the rock planting is usually displayed in a flat water basin or a tray filled with fine sand. Because the rocks here are meant to denote mountains, they are invariably placed vertically—for dramatic effect—rather than horizontally.

Pines, junipers, spruces, larches, and cotoneasters are ideal subjects for planting in this style.

Detail of the roots. Notice how they have grown tightly around the rock. When the tree was first imported, the roots were badly marked by wire used in training, but over the years the wire marks have disappeared and the tree now looks very natural.

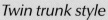
Twin trunk style

MULTIPLE TRUNK STYLES

The twin trunk style features two trunks with the fork starting from fairly low down the tree. A twin trunk style will not be effective if the second trunk starts too far up the main tree. Trees which fork naturally from the base make ideal twin trunk bonsai. They may be created by either air-layering a forked branch of a mature tree or by using nursery or collected material. In this style, the two trunks must never be exactly the same height as the tree would then look incongruous. It is usual for one trunk to be considerably shorter than the other.

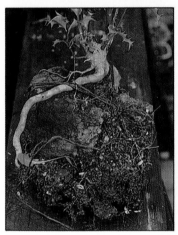

If the subsidiary trunk is much shorter than the main trunk then this composition is referred to as the "mother and son" style. If the second trunk is only a little shorter than the main trunk, then it is referred to by the Chinese as the "mother and daughter" style. Needless to say, this style of bonsai looks very natural as trees are often seen growing in this fashion in the wild. Although the tree has two trunks the overall shape of a twin trunk bonsai is basically conical. Branches should not cross, and branches between the two trunks should not grow into each other.

Above: English holly (*Ilex aquifofium*) being trained over a piece of rock for use either as a root-over-rock or as an exposed root style bonsai. The roots have to be tied very tightly to the rock at all times.

Above left: This ivy has grown from a cutting I took twenty one years ago and is being trained for the planted on rock style.

Triple trunk style

The triple trunk style is very similar to the twin trunk style, the only difference being that there are three instead of two trunks. The main trunk is usually the tallest and centrally located with the two subsidiary trunks on either side. The subsidiary trunks do not have to be the same height as each other, neither does the tallest trunk have to be the central one—there are many different compositions all pleasing to the eye. Air-layerings and collected trees are a good source for this style of bonsai.

Above: Group planting of seven Chamaecyparis pisifera "Boulevard" (Sawara cypress). The tree not fully visible stands directly behind the second tree on the left, and the tallest is 35 in (90 cm). The source material was ordinary garden center stock.

Opposite top right: This trident maple bonsai has been grown over a piece of rock for the last four years to develop a root-over-rock style tree.

Above: A group of nine Japanese larches planted on a lovely piece of slate. The oldest tree is about twenty years old and 30 in (80 cm) high. Most trees in this group bear cones regularly. Trees planted on slate or flat pieces of rock are usually started off in ordinary seed trays. They are lifted out and placed on slate when the roots have filled the tray completely. This usually takes one growing season.

Multiple trunk style

Again this is basically similar to the two previous styles except that there are many more trunks which emanate from the base. Trees which have been "stooled" (i.e. cut down at the base each year) are a useful source for multiple trunk bonsai.

Root connected style

This is sometimes referred to as the raft, sinuous, or straight line style. In this style of bonsai, all the individual trees are in fact branches from one main tree, but have over the years been trained to resemble individual trees. However, they will all still be connected to each other by a single common horizontal root.

This style of bonsai is very similar to a group or forest planting except that the "individual" trees are not really separate. There seems to be no real point in creating the group effect by this method except that it is an unusual horticultural technique. Junipers, pines, and trident maples lend themselves

to this method of development because they all produce roots very easily from the trunks. In the wild, many of the common junipers tend to grow in this fashion. When the trees get too large they fall over and rest on the peaty soil. Fallen trunks and branches in time send roots down into the soil and the small subsidiary branches effectively become separate trees. This style of bonsai is once again a direct copy from nature.

MULTIPLE TREE OR GROUP STYLES

Group planting

The group or forest planting style is one of the most natural looking of bonsai styles. A beautifully composed group can and ought to convey the essence of a real forest. A group planting derives its realistic appearance from the sense of perspective created by using different sized trees. Perspective is also created by positioning trees skilfully in relation both to the container and to each other. Group plantings closely echo trees depicted in landscape paintings. Just as many books have been written on landscape painting, so volumes could be written about group plantings.

Group plantings can be made from relatively immature trees, or trees which have little potential as individual specimens. In Japan, trees which have limited possibilities are sometimes referred to as "trees suitable for group planting". The aesthetic design of a group planting can be a very sophisticated matter. Space plays a critical part in the design. Expanses of empty space either to the left or the right of the composition can create a feeling of scale which belies the actual size of the trees used in the group. A group composed almost entirely of large thick-trunked trees produces a feeling of proximity to a forest. The Japanese sometimes refer to this as the "near view" style of group planting. Predominantly slim-trunked trees grouped en masse (usually over 21 trees) create the illusion of being far away from a forest. The Japanese refer to this as the "distant view" style of group planting. Of course, trees of different sizes may also be used to great effect within a single group.

Tradition dictates that for groups with fewer than eleven trees an uneven number of trees should be used. This tradition has an aesthetic basis in that numbers such as three, five, and seven are relatively easy to arrange, especially when triangular shapes and asymmetrical designs are involved. Those who have experience of flower arranging will be familiar with this concept. This balance and harmony are more difficult to obtain using even numbers. The Chinese never use four trees in a group as this is supposed to bring bad luck. The number four in Chinese means death and it is therefore avoided like the plague!

The trees in a group or forest planting do not have to be grouped tightly together. Two or even three small clumps in a

Below: This group of five Hinoki cypress was imported from Japan twenty-five years ago. On a piece of sandstone, the group is 22 in (55 cm) high and 36 in (90 cm) across. It is extremely heavy because the rock alone weighs nearly 66lbs (30 kg). The foliage has to be thinned regularly in order to prevent die-back of the lower branches.

single composition often add a singular charm and vitality quite different from that of a single massed group.

Group plantings are repotted in very much the same way that individual trees are repotted. The roots from the edges of the group are teased out, trimmed off, and fresh soil introduced. If certain trees within the group have become too large or have died off, it may be necessary to rearrange the entire planting or even to start again from scratch.

An example of the multiple tree on rock style using Chinese junipers and carboniferous limestone. The trees manage to survive on very little soil. They are, however, fed regularly with liquid fertilizer. The entire composition is 33 in (85 cm) high, the rock in this case weighing 99lbs (45 kg). It is not easy to transport this group to shows.

Multiple tree on rock style

Group plantings may sometimes be placed on flat pieces of slate or rock instead of in a shallow container, and this can look very beautiful and natural too. Several trees can also be planted on a vertical plane on an interesting piece of rock to convey the sense of growing out of a cliff face as is often seen in Chinese paintings.

The points to remember in creating this style of group planting are (a) keep the scale of tree and rock in proper

A small bonsai of *Pinus sylvestris repens*. It is only 8 in (20 cm) high and was created from ordinary nursery stock. The graft is rather too high, but by careful paring of the union the trunk could be improved. Nevertheless, this tree has great potential.

proportion, and (b) leave the beautiful parts of the rock exposed to view.

Smallish trees are best for this style and they need to be fairly drought-resistant. Pieces of copper wire anchored in epoxy resin allow the roots of the trees to be safely secured to the rock. A fairly loamy compost is necessary in order to retain as much moisture as possible. The trees for this type of planting are usually started off in small pots and once properly established, they are transferred to the rock and secured to it by the wire. There is no real mystique to making plantings of this kind. All that is needed is some ingenuity and a bit of common sense.

Landscape style

The art of sai-kei or *pen-jing* is a subject in its own right. The scope for creativity is absolutely immense because the limiting factor here is simply the artist's own imagination. Tray or potted landscapes are not regarded by some purists as proper bonsai, but they nonetheless have an important place in the historical and cultural evolution of bonsai.

Miniature Chinese gardens have been created from the very earliest times, based on mountains and other natural features of the landscape. One development in Chinese garden art was that of growing miniature trees or bonsai as we know them today; another was *pen-jing* or potted landscape.

In *pen-jing* there are no pretensions. Rocks denote mountains and miniature trees represent real trees growing in the wild. The juxtaposition of these various elements conveys the feeling of the appropriate scale, and the entire composition comes alive. Miniature ceramic figures of men, houses, and boats lend further interest and are deployed principally to emphasize scale. That these compositions look realistic cannot be denied and it is not difficult to understand the attractions of *pen-jing* and sai-kei. In bonsai the size of sai-kei or *pen-jing* compositions is irrelevant. As long as the proportions are correct, the feeling of realism will have been achieved.

Classification of bonsai by size

To the layman, one bonsai is very much like another. To the connoisseur however every bonsai is quite different. Not only are there different styles of bonsai, but different sizes too. Bonsai range from 2 in (5 cm 5 cm) high to over 6 ft (2 m). The following sizes are commonly recognized in the bonsai world.

Less than 2 in (5 cm)	thimble or thumb size bonsai
2-6 in (5-15cm)	*mame* or miniature bonsai
6-12 in (15-30cm)	small bonsai
12-24 in (30-60 cm)	medium size bonsai
24-48 in (60-120 cm)	big bonsai
Over 4 ft (120 cm)	very large bonsai

In Japan, trees over 4 ft (120 cm) are not considered bonsai because the term bonsai is intended to cover only miniature trees. In China potted trees are often grown well over 10 ft (3 m) tall and though they are really dwarf trees they are nevertheless very beautiful.

It should be emphasized that the classification of bonsai by size can only be arbitrary. There are no hard and fast rules.

The Taoist influence on bonsai has been very significant.
In the early days bonsai and magic were closely
intertwined.

CHAPTER 6

BASIC HORTICULTURAL PRINCIPLES

Bonsai trees are like human beings in many ways. They need food, air, and water to keep them alive, and lots of love to keep them happy. The trees are, however, also totally dependent on light. Unfortunately, this is not often appreciated by the beginner, and the bonsai which started off either as a present or an impulse purchase soon ends up as a dead tree. There is no excuse for not being able to keep a tree alive and healthy. As long as certain basic principles are followed a tree should live to a ripe old age. One simply needs to remember that a bonsai requires the four essentials—water, light, air, and food. Of the four basic ingredients, water is perhaps the most important; then comes light, next air, and finally food.

Water

A bonsai is almost totally dependent on man for its supply of water; rain cannot be relied on as the sole source of water for bonsai. During a hot summer, rain can be infrequent or irregular. During the growing season a bonsai must be watered daily. If watering is neglected for any reason the tree could suffer irreparable damage. Even if watering is missed for only a day, the leaves can all shrivel up. Daily watering of bonsai is essential mainly because the containers in which the trees grow are so small. The smallness of the root ball makes it very difficult for the soil to act as a reservoir for water for any prolonged period of time. During the summer it is vital that the tree is watered at least once, if not twice, on very hot days. Watering in the evening is perhaps the best time, but if a twice-daily watering regime is necessary then watering should be done once in the early morning and again in the evening. Watering should ideally be done with rainwater using a watering can fitted with a fine rose. If rainwater is not available, tapwater that has been left to stand in a bin or bucket for over twenty-four hours should be used. If there are too many trees to water using a watering can, a hosepipe is the next best solution, although this is by no means ideal. Tapwater can be harmful if it is very hard, i.e. if it contains a lot of lime. Correct watering might appear to be a very straightforward matter but it is not as easy as one might imagine. It is very much an art in the cultivation of bonsai. A tree should be watered just enough to keep it in good health. Over-watering is as harmful as under-watering.

When watering a tree, always water from above to simulate a fine shower of rain. Water the leaves as well as the soil around the base of the tree. Water the soil until the water begins to trickle out of the drainage holes in the bottom of the pot. Return after approximately ten minutes and repeat the watering operation once.

If a tree is healthy and growing strongly and the soil mix is just right, over-watering will not do it any great harm.

However, if a tree is not properly established (e.g. if it has just been repotted) then watering should be very carefully controlled. A sick tree should never be over-watered as it could get waterlogged and die.

During the winter, when a tree is resting and there is a lot of damp and moisture about, there is no need to water unless the tree has been placed in a covered shelter. In these circumstances, keep a careful eye on the soil. The general rule for winter care is that a tree should not need to be watered if kept in the open, and only occasional watering to keep the soil damp if kept under cover.

Regular watering must begin in early spring and continue right through to the end of the growing season in the fall. Never water during the middle of the day when the sun is shining strongly on the plant. The water droplets on the leaves can act as burning glasses and cause scorch marks as they catch the sun.

Light

Light is absolutely essential for the well-being of plants and trees. Without it, plants would not be able to produce the food they need to stay alive. Plants harness the energy in sunlight to transform the carbon dioxide they extract from the air, and water they draw from the soil, to produce carbohydrate in their leaf tissues. This complex process is called photosynthesis and involves the manufacture of sugars by linking the carbon atoms (from carbon dioxide) together in a series of chemical reactions. Its most valuable by-product is the oxygen we breathe.

The importance of light cannot be over-emphasized. Bonsai should be grown in full sunlight as far as possible. There are, of course, some varieties of trees which cannot stand strong sunlight, but trees should not as a rule be grown under shading or kept indoors. They must have as much light as possible so that the leaves can photosynthesize in order to produce food for the tree. The leaves of the more delicate species such as maples and beech, which can get scorched by strong direct sunlight, should be given some protection. This can be provided by partial shading in the form of overhead netting.

Most evergreens, as a rule, like full sun. All the pines and junipers thrive in full sunshine. The Hinoki and Sawara cypresses, however, prefer partial shade in mid-summer. Most deciduous trees can stand full sun during the early summer but in mid-summer, when the sun is really strong, they appreciate partial shade. Evergreen trees should not be kept under cover during the winter. They can be left outdoors or if the weather is very severe they can be kept in a cool greenhouse. Deciduous trees which will have lost all their leaves can of course be kept in dark conditions.

Air

Air is, of course, the source of carbon dioxide which is needed by plants to produce food and it is just as important in the soil because tree roots, like leaves, need to breathe. If soil air is excluded, as happens when soil is waterlogged, the roots suffocate and the tree will eventually die. The millions of microorganisms that live in the soil also need air; without it they too die and the soil becomes putrid and lifeless.

Soil

Most plants need soil in order to grow. Soil is perhaps the most important raw material after water. Soil is made up of two ingredients, organic and inorganic matter. The organic material, which is called humus, is derived from vegetable and animal matter. The inorganic material comes from weathered rock. Different soils have differing amounts of humus and rocky substances. The geology of a region determines to a large extent the nature of the soil. Soils in a predominantly limestone region will be alkaline. Where the geology is igneous, orvolcanic, the soil will be slightly acidic.

The size of the soil particles determines whether a soil is predominantly clay, loam, or sand . Soil that is made up predominantly of very fine particles is called clay, those that are predominantly composed of medium-size grains are known as silt, while those that have the largest particles are called sand. Agood loamy soil has just the right mix of clay and sand.

The spaces between the soil particles trap air, and this is often referred to as the atmosphere in soil. The soil atmosphere plays a most important role in plant development. The roots of plants all require air in order to breathe, and if air is not available the plant cannot grow. It should also be remembered that a soil will have in it millions of microorganisms and these organisms will need a constant supply of air and water in order to survive.

There are some who advocate the sterilization of soils used for bonsai. This practice is highly dubious in my view because more harm than good can come of it. Sterilizing soil kills all the beneficial bacteria and other microorganisms, leaving the soil virtually lifeless. Soil needs these microorganisms in order to break down the humus and thereby release the beneficial chemical elements. These elements are essential for healthy plant development. There is therefore no need to sterilize soil. If a bonsai is healthy to begin with, the risk of disease infestation through the soil is minimal.

A good basic formula for bonsai soil is one-third sphagnum moss peat, one-third sand, and one-third ordinary garden loam. This recipe should be suitable for most varieties of trees but it can be varied slightly for trees with special requirements.

Pines, for instance, prefer a sandy soil, and older pines in particular prefer a soil which is almost 50% sand or grit. Most flowering trees prefer a rich loamy soil to which farmyard manure or stable manure has been added. Deciduous trees generally prefer more loam and humus in the soil.

A soil should have adequate moisture without being soaking wet. The texture of an ideal bonsai soil is such that it should be possible to squeeze a handful together without it either crumbling apart or oozing water. It should be slightly springy in texture.

Fertilizer requirements

A common misconception about bonsai is that they are deliberately starved of food and nutrients in order to keep them dwarfed. There is a certain logic in this argument, but it does not reflect the way bonsai are grown. Bonsai may be small, but they are otherwise healthy and vigorous trees. The dwarfing process is not achieved by starving, but by constant trimming of the foliage, and by the restriction of root development. Because bonsai grow in fairly confined spaces soil nutrient availability is that much more limited. That is why these trees need to be fertilized fairly regularly. Although the soil in which the tree is growing will contain a fair amount of nutrients, these may not be correctly balanced. A regular and balanced feeding progamme is therefore absolutely essential.

What kind of "food" does a bonsai require? Certainly not a diet of beef steak or hamburgers! The nutrients required by bonsai are no different from those needed by ordinary plants and trees. Six basic chemical elements are needed in fairly large quantities to maintain a plant's health and vitality. They are nitrogen (N), phosphorus (P), potassium (K), calcium (Ca), sulfur (S) and magnesium (Mg). The other elements also necessary for plant development are the "trace elements", iron (Fe), manganese (Mn), copper (Cu), and boron (B) etc. These trace elements are needed only in minute quantities. As a plant grows it extracts the nutrients from the soil and they must therefore be replaced from time to time. Different plants and trees take up these elements in differing quantities. The uptake of the different elements may also vary according to the age of the tree. Young and old trees can require the same elements in quite different proportions.

Organic and inorganic fertilizers

Plant nutrients are supplied artificially in the form of fertilizer. This may be organic i.e. natural material derived from animal or vegetable sources or inorganic i.e. derived from mineral sources.

Inorganic or chemical fertilizers can be made up to different formulae to suit the differing feeding requirements of various plant varieties. Some plants require more nitrogen than others, while others require more potassium or phosphorus. The feeding requirements also vary with the time of year. Thus, in spring, most plants and trees as a rule need a lot of nitrogen to promote leaf growth. As the year progresses, more phosphorus and potassium will be needed to help flower bud and fruit development. It is also needed to harden the wood. Inorganic fertilizers provide a very convenient means of varying the different elements which go to make up a balanced fertilizer. Hence the great variety of fertilizers on the market. There are those which promote leaf growth, and others that promote flowering and fruiting on shrubs and trees. The choice can be quite bewildering.

It is important to understand how fertilizers work if the trees and plants are to derive the maximum benefit from their use. You need to know what nitrogen, for instance, does for plants, and what special properties phosphorus and potassium possess in a fertilizer. A brief explanation of the roles of the various elements is useful in this connection.

The nitrogen (N) content in inorganic fertilizers is usually provided by ammonium or nitrate compounds. Ammonium nitrate, ammonium sulfate, and calcium nitrate are the compounds most often used for supplying nitrogen . Organic fertilizers rich in nitrogen are hop manure, dried blood, and crushed hoof and horn.

Phosphorus (P) is usually obtained from superphosphate or muriate of potash . Most of this comes from north Africa where it is mined on an extensive scale. Some of the Pacific islands are also a rich source of superphosphate. These deposits have been formed over centuries from millions of tons of bird droppings. It is not surprising, therefore, that this should be such a rich source of fertilizer. A fertilizer that contains phosphorus will very often have potassium (K) as well. When these two elements occur together in a fertilizer, it is referred to as a "PK" fertilizer. A brand of "PK" fertilizer which is highly beneficial for trees is called En Mag. It is extensively used in forestry practice and is ideal for bonsai.

Magnesium (Mg) is usually derived from Epsom salts (magnesium sulfate). Epsom salts is a very quick-acting fertilizer. Trees and plants suffering from magnesium deficiency are usually a sickly yellow color. A single application of Epsom salts on a tree suffering from this deficiency can do wonders for it.

Organic fertilizers such as hop manure and the different animal manures vary considerably in their chemical composition. Hop manure is rich in nitrogen but low in potassium while farmyard manure is very rich in potassium but low in nitrogen. Organic fertilizers are used not so much for their nutrient value but for the improvement to soil structure which the organic matter provides. This is not to say that they are of no value as

a source of chemical nutrients. Organic fertilizers are also a very valuable source of "mycorrhizal" fungi. These fungi grow in close association with the roots of most tree species. The fungi and tree roots interact with each other to provide mutual benefit. The mycorrhizas help the host plant by improving its ability to absorb minerals from the soil and also confer greater disease resistance. The plant in return provides the fungi with a copious supply of food and other nutrients.

Many bonsai growers now recognize the value of mycorrhiza in their soil and transfer it (from pine bonsai which are already well established) to soil planted with bonsai so that it can multiply during the growing season . Like most fungi they exude a lovely aroma of mushrooms.

Although fertilizers are generally beneficial to plants, they can do considerable harm if applied wrongly. Over-application has the effect of "burning" the leaves and the roots and can cause death. If there is too much fertilizer in the soil, it will draw water out of the plant which will become quite unable to assimilate water. The lack of water would soon turn the leaves brown and the tree would succumb.

Fertilizers for bonsai should be applied carefully and sparingly. Bonsai are smaller than ordinary trees and therefore much more vulnerable to the effects of over-feeding. The golden rule to follow is half the recommended fertilizer strength every time a bonsai is fed . It is always better to give several applications of a weak dose rather than a single application of a full strength dose.

Inorganic fertilizers are sold in two basic forms-solid and liquid. The solid fertilizers come in the form of powders or granules, while liquid fertilizers are usually concentrated solutions of chemicals mixed in water. Chemical fertilizers should not, as a rule, be mixed in bonsai soil unless they are of the slow release type. Fertilizers mixed in soil for potting up could burn the roots.

Fertilizers may be applied from early spring for evergreens and from mid-spring onwards in the case of deciduous trees. A weak application should be given every fortnight for more vigorous trees. Older established trees require less feeding. Bonsai are like people in this respect. Just as young growing children need more food than adults, so in the same way, young trees need to be fed more often than older trees. A good way to remember a feeding schedule is to fix it on set days each month, e.g. the first and the fourteenth days, or the first and third Sundays.

In spring and early summer, a high-nitrogen fertilizer is beneficial to most trees. From mid-summer onwards a low-nitrogen and high-PK fertilizer should be used in order to harden the wood and to induce fruiting and flowering.

If you are using a liquid fertilizer, place the tree in a drip tray so that none of the fertilizer is wasted. Whatever the form of the fertilizer (whether powder, granular, or liquid) always water the tree before applying it. The best time of day to do this is

very early morning before the sun shines on the foliage, or late in the evening after watering. Never apply fertilizer at midday or in the scorching sun.

Pests and diseases

Bonsai are susceptible to attacks from pests and diseases in very much the same way that other plants and trees are. However, because a bonsai is relatively small the problem of pest control and eradication is much simpler. For this reason bonsai have a better chance of good health than their full size relations and may enjoy great longevity.

Plant diseases are caused mainly by fungi. The following are some of the more common diseases encountered in the temperate zone.

Rust

Many forms of rust attack both coniferous and broad-leaved trees. The symptoms can be identified by the yellow- or orange-colored spots and blisters which appear on the leaves. Trees commonly affected by rust are oak, birch, alder, Scots pine, European five-needle pine, larch, and juniper. Rust is difficult to control although copper fungicide and Benomyl can prevent the disease from spreading. Affected leaves should be burnt.

Needle cast (Lophodermium seditiosum) on pines

This disease affects mainly the Scots and the European pines, although Asian pines are also vulnerable. The symptoms appear on the pine needles as little brown spots about $\frac{1}{4}$-$\frac{1}{2}$ in (0.5-1 mm) in diameter interspersed with thin black lines. The disease affects mainly young needles, although older needles are also vulnerable. The diseased needles are shed during the fall when normally only the older needles fall. A very severe attack of needle cast may completely defoliate a tree, but it can be controlled with Benomyl, Maneb, or Zineb. European larches are also susceptible to needle cast, although the guilty fungus is a different one. The symptoms are fairly similar and Zineb is the most effective fungicide.

Gray mold

Most gardeners will be familiar with this disease. The fungus is encouraged by dead leaves and overcrowded growing

Opposite above left: Very little can be done about the sudden wilting caused by verticillium wilt, except to maintain clean growing conditions. *Center:* Pine needle rust results in premature needle loss but can be controlled by winter spraying with lime sulfur. Right: Scale insects are very common but can be effectively treated with malathion or diazinon.

Opposite below left: Winter moth larvae are particularly pernicious in the spring, eating new growth, but can be controlled with gamma BHC. Center: Gall affects leaves and stems: these should be removed as sprays are not usually effective. *Right:* Common spangle gall affects oaks but is more unsightly than detrimental. Kelthane and lime sulfur are both effective treatments.

Right: Contrary to popular belief, bonsai are not starved in order to keep them dwarfed. They are in fact fed regularly in order to keep them in prime condition. Fertilizer may be applied in granular, powder, or liquid form. Here a powder fertilizer is being applied to a Chinese juniper. Notice the bright green foliage: a sure sign of a healthy tree.

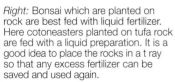

Right: Bonsai which are planted on rock are best fed with liquid fertilizer. Here cotoneasters planted on tufa rock are fed with a liquid preparation. It is a good idea to place the rocks in a t ray so that any excess fertilizer can be saved and used again.

conditions. It attacks young growth in deciduous and coniferous trees. Young maple seedlings are particularly prone to attack, larches, cypresses, and cryptomeria only slightly less so. Benomyl and Captan are the most effective fungicides.

Oak mildew

The symptoms are similar to those of Gray mold and young oak leaves are particularly susceptible. Oak mildew should be treated with Benomyl and Dinocap.

Damping off of seedlings

If damping off has been a problem in the past, then freshly sown seeds should be soaked with Captanor Cheshunt compound solution.

Verticillium wilt

This disease affects most Acer species. It manifests itself when trees suddenly wilt or die for no obvious reason . Trident maples growing in the ground are prone to this type of wilt. The disease can usually be confirmed when the stem or trunk of a dead tree is cut open. The affected part will have longitudinal dark brown bands running through it. The only way to get rid of this disease is to dig up the plant bed and fumigate the soil.

General note

It is always a good idea to spray all trees with Benomyl at the start of the growing season to kill off any spores which have overwintered. Regular spraying with Benomyl, Captan, and Maneb at monthly intervals will help to suppress most of the common tree diseases. Prevention is always better than cure.

Insect pests

Insect pests not only cause physical damage but they can badly disfigure bonsai. There are three main groups of insect pests : borers, which feed on roots and stems; leaf cutters, which also feed on roots and stems; and leaf and stem suckers such as aphids and scale insects.

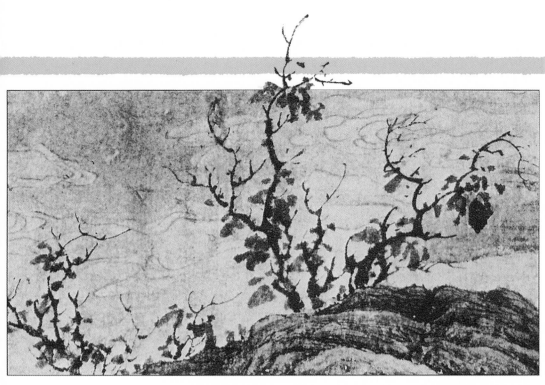

Most borers are larvae of moths, weevils, and beetles which hide in the ground or in the trunks and branches of trees. They must be watched for carefully throughout the year. Leaf cutters are active mainly during the summer months and cause a great deal of damage to leaves. Scale insects attack leaves and young shoots by sucking the sap. Most insect pests can be eradicated by using any of the proprietary insecticides on the market. Most of them contain one or more of the following chemicals: diazinon, gamma BHC, fenitrothion, and malathion.

As in the case of fungicides, insecticides should be sprayed on bonsai at regular intervals throughout the year to kill both newly laid eggs and young grubs virtually invisible to the naked eye. Always spray either very early in the morning or in the evening after the trees have been watered. Insecticides and fungicides must be handled very carefully since many of them are hazardous to pets, fish, bees, and people. They should always be kept out of reach of children.

Herbicides

Bonsai enthusiasts who have large collections of trees may find herbicides useful for controlling weeds. Herbicides are also a great help in nursery and growing beds where trees are grown for making into bonsai . The two herbicides which are most commonly used in this connection are simazine and paraquat.

Simazine may be in either granular or liquid form, while paraquat is applied only in liquid form. Simazine is extremely effective as a pre-emergent weed killer when applied in early spring and late fall. Paraquat is most effective when weeds are growing strongly in the spring and throughout the summer.

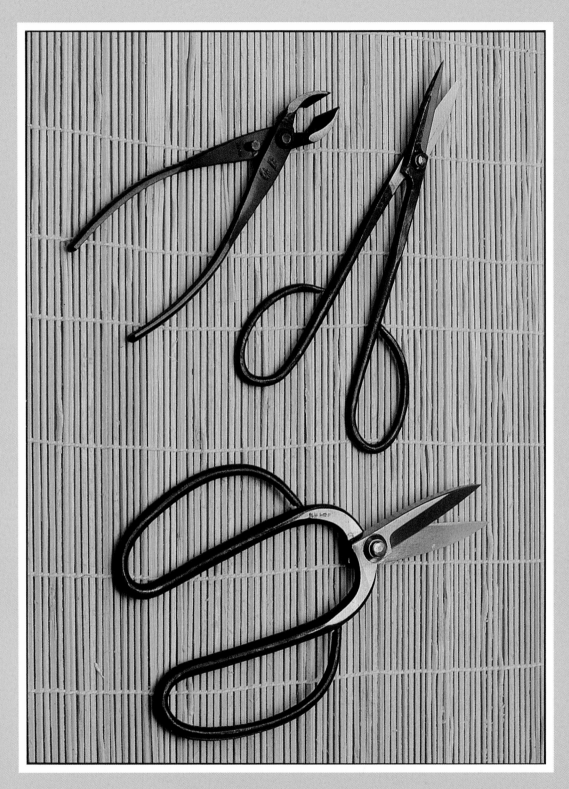

The three most useful bonsai tools. The tool at the top left is a concave branch cutter used for removing branches. The curved blades enable complete removal of branches without leaving any snags. The tool at the top right is a long-handled twig cutter and is handy for cutting off unwanted or dead branches from inside the foliage canopy The tool at the bottom is a long-bladed shears or scissors. This is a general trimming tool and also extremely useful for pruning roots.

HARDWARE

In today's "do-it-yourself" society, most people appreciate the importance of having the proper tools for the job. Just as there are special tools for the car, so in bonsai there are specific tools for performing specific tasks. However, it would be quite wrong to give the impression that all of them are absolutely essential for making a bonsai. After all, the early Chinese managed with just a few basic implements. There is no denying though, that having the right tools certainly helps. Some enthusiasts go to the extreme and acquire almost every tool that is available, but their bonsai may be no better for it. A happy medium must be struck.

The basic bonsai tool kit need only be a bonsai branch pruner, a pair of short-handled scissors, and a pair of long-handled scissors. Most of the other tools can be improvised from common garden implements. Not included in the bonsai tool list are things such as a garden fork and shovel, or a sieve and a watering can. These are items which most gardeners would possess anyway.

By far the most useful tool is the concave branch cutter. This tool is almost like a surgical instrument because it is extremely sharp and precise. It can cut right up to the trunk of the tree leaving no snag at all. A clean cut also helps prevent disease infestation. Ordinary pruning shears are inadequate as they cannot be brought close enough to the trunk. The second most useful bonsai tool is a pair of short-handled (long-bladed) scissors. This tool is very useful for general trimming, but its greatest value is for trimming roots at repotting time. The third most important tool is a pair of long-handled (short-bladed) scissors. This tool is most convenient for probing deep into the branch structure of a mature tree and is used for cutting fine branches and twigs. It is also an extremely useful tool for leaf pruning.

For teasing roots during repotting a three-pronged cultivator, made by most gardening tool firms, is extremely useful. It is much more useful than the traditional chopstick or even the bonsai rake, which very often is not strong enough for the job.

A turntable made from an old office chair, or even a piece of board mounted on three castors, is quite indispensable when it comes to wiring and shaping. The other option, of course, is to purchase expensive equipment, but it is worth remembering that most implements can be improvised from cast-offs and other old artifacts.

Care of tools

Tools will last a very long time if given proper care. It always pays to keep tools clean and free from rust. After using a tool it is a good idea to wipe it over with an oily rag. Tools that have been used to cut dead wood, or wood which has signs of disease, should be sterilized using a weak solution of sterilizing

fluid to minimize the risk of spreading the disease. Any proprietary sterilizer or disinfectant will do. All cutting tools should be sharpened regularly with an oil stone. This is particularly important for chisels used for carving wood and for branch cutters and scissors. Never drop these tools on stone or concrete as this may cause irreparable damage. A plastic tool caddy or shoe shine box is handy for carrying tools around.

A watering can, preferably with a very fine rose, is another indispensable piece of equipment and apart from its obvious use can also serve as a container for mixing fertilizer. A metal watering can with a long spout and brass rose is ideal for bonsai work. Not only is this type of can extremely hard-wearing, but it is also easy to handle as it is well balanced. It is not a good idea to keep water standing permanently in a can since algae will soon develop and clog up the rose.

Other tools which are useful for bonsai, though not essential, are large and small pruning saws. These could be either the small folding saw or the large bow-type pruning saw. A chain saw also has its uses when it comes to tackling large commercial trees.

A power drill is also a very useful tool for bonsai. It can be used for drilling holes in various parts of a tree to create the impression of age. It can also be used with a flexible drive for carving implements, polishing tools, routers, and buffers.

A blowlamp is another very useful tool for melting grafting wax. It is always handy to have one around.

Wire

The use of wire in bonsai is a fairly recent innovation and it has already become quite indispensable to the contemporary bonsai artist. It is difficult to imagine what bonsai practitioners used in the days before wire was introduced, but they must have found shaping quite difficult without it. The Chinese preferred to use the "clip and grow" method which did not entail the use of wire at all, but the aesthetic effect is not quite the same. There is little doubt that wiring is a great asset to bonsai. Almost any shape can be created by using wire skilfully.

In the inter-war years, ordinary iron wire was used extensively in Japan. It is still used widely for mass-produced commercial bonsai but it has been replaced to a large extent by copper wire since the Second World War. Much more recently, within the last five years or so, copper wire has been replaced by anodized aluminum wire for both technical and cost reasons. Modern aluminum wire is much more pliable and relatively inert—it does not have the disadvantage of reacting with water, soil, or fertilizer. There is no reason why traditional copper wire may not be used, particularly as it is

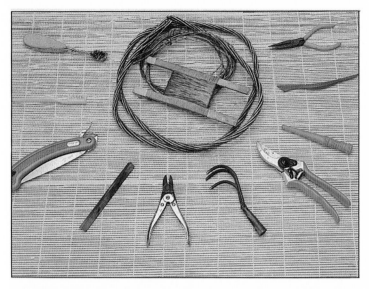

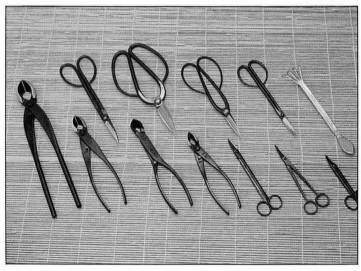

Top: A selection of tools and implements useful for bonsai. *Counterclockwise from top left:* The wire brush and toothbrush on the left are very useful for cleaning driftwood. The saw is indispensable for cutting larger branches. The oilstone is used for sharpening scissors, cutters and pruning shears. The wire cutters are used for cutting training wire. The three-pronged cultivator is ideal for teasing out roots when repotting. Good quality secateurs are essential for general pruning work. The dibble comes in handy for striking cuttings and for general potting up. The pliers are used for jinning.

Above: Chisels can be used to create special effects on trunks. The top row shows ordinary woodworking chisels below which are special bonsai carving tools.

much easier to obtain than the special anodized aluminum wire. Single-core PVC-coated copper cable may also be used for training bonsai. The PVC covering need not in fact be removed as it protects the branches that are being wired from permanent disfigurement. The disadvantage of course is that PVC-coated wire is unslightly, especially if it is brightly colored. However, if a tree is merely in training and not for exhibition it hardly matters if the wires are visible at this stage.

Copper wire should be annealed by heating it in a bonfire of newspaper. The heat from this is usually sufficient to make it more pliable. Some hobby and craft shops sell copper wire by weight in reels. Alternatively, you can buy copper wire already stripped and cleaned from scrap merchants. Green plastic-covered galvanized wire may also be used and this is easily obtained from most hardware stores and garden shops. The proper aluminum anodized wire for bonsai work can only be purchased from bonsai nurseries. It is more expensive than ordinary copper wire, but well worth it because it is so much easier to use. It is also usable over and over again.

Top: A chain saw has many uses in bonsai cultivation. It can be used as a rough carving tool on large t ru nks and can also be used for cutting off large branches. The mUlti-purpose drill is an asset when it comes to refin ing jins and large driftwood areas on specimen trees. These are just some of the implements which I use for carving both live and dead wood on bonsai.

Above: AA selection of different sized branch cutters, scissors, and trimming tools. The tool on the top row (far right) is a small rake and spatula combined.

Pots

The pot or container for the tree is naturally an integral part of a bonsai. Pots come in all different shapes and sizes. They range from thimble size pots to some which are made for trees over 6 ft (2 m) high. Traditional bonsai pots are made of ceramic material, usually stoneware clay. Stoneware pots are used because they are frost-proof and relatively cheap. Some pots are made from porcelain , but they are rather more expensive. Pots which are made from red or white earthenware clay (such as is used for making ordinary tableware) are not recommended for use in temperate climates since they soon crack in the frost. Plastic pots can be bought but they have not proved to be very popular because they are not as durable as stoneware pots.

Pots are to bonsai as clothes are to people. A bonsai pot can literally alter the appearance of a tree. Like clothes, pots have been subject to changes in fashion . At the turn of the twentieth century, it was fashionable to use deep round bonsai pots. These were often highly decorative and made from porcelain. In recent years shallower pots have become the vogue.

A bonsai pot must have good drainage or else its value for bonsai will be extremely limited. The larger and the more numerous the holes the better. A good pot should not have areas within it which trap water, since otherwise the roots would soon rot. Aside from the technical factors, the choice of pot is basically an aesthetic decision.

There are some pots that have no holes. They are called water-basins, *sui-poon* or sui-ban and are used almost exclusively for displaying rock landscapes or *sui-seki*, water stones.

Fibreglass is sometimes used for making very large pots where lightness and strength are important factors. For the ordinary DIY enthusiast, concrete pots can be extremely attractive as an alternative to proper ceramic ones.

These antique Chinese bonsai pots are part of my collection of bonsai paraphernalia. They are made of porcelain and are all about one hundred years old; the octagonal pot in the center is about 16 in (40 cm) in diameter. The stands too are antique.

Plants and shrubs have been cultivated by the Chinese
and Japanese for thousands of years. It is hardly
surprising that bonsai should have originated in the East.

CHAPTER 8

CULTIVATION TECHNIQUES

Above:.This is the wrong way to cut a branch. The cut should never be parallel to the main trunk.

Top: There is a right way and a wrong way to use branch pruners. The right way is to approach the branch from the side, not from the bottom or top. The cutting blades should be at right-angles to the main trunk line.

Bonsai is a curious mixture of horticulture and art. A good understanding of horticultural principles provides a firm basis on which to start this hobby, but to this must be added artistic flair. The earlier chapters have described various methods of starting a bonsai, the varieties of suitable trees, the definition of various classical styles, and the essential horticultural principles. The special techniques necessary to transform ordinary trees and shrubs into bonsai remain to be revealed.

Branch pruning

Pruning is an absolutely basic bonsai practice. It would be quite impossible to create bonsai without resorting to some kind of pruning. Most beginners are afraid to prune, imagining that the plant would be damaged or killed by such action. This worry is natural and not unlike the fear of water people experience when they first learn to swim. The problem for the bonsai artist is not so much knowing how to prune, but what to prune and when.

There is no mystique in using a pair of pruning shears or branch pruners. All you need to remember is that the cut must be made cleanly. The pruning shears should be kept sharp and free from dirt. A pair of good quality pruning shears is a great asset for general pruning work, while a pair of concave branch cutters is really indispensable. This tool enables cuts to be made right up to the trunk leaving no snags behind. There is a right and a wrong way to prune. Cuts should always be made at right angles to the branch or trunk which is being retained . Cuts should never be made parallel to the main trunk or branch as there is a real risk of tearing the bark or cambium. Approaching a branch at right angles ensures a neat cut.

A sharp saw is another valuable tool for bonsai and can be employed to remove thick branches which ordinary pruning shears are unable to cut through. As with all tools, saws need to be kept sharp and clean so that they cut smartly and do not transmit disease. When using a saw to cut a branch, cut from the underside first to a point half-way through the branch, and then cut the rest of the branch from the top. This method further reduces the risks of tearing the bark and cambium.

Pruning is always a drastic procedure and should therefore be done very carefully. Timing is crucial. As a general guide, the best time to prune is when the sap is not rising in the tree. This makes the dormant season the ideal time for pruning. Late fall is the best time to prune pines. Other evergreens such as junipers prefer to be pruned in the winter or early spring. Most deciduous trees prefer to be pruned during late winter or early spring when the dormant buds are just beginning to break. Japanese maples should certainly not be pruned in early spring because the sap will be rising very strongly, but rather in mid-winter when there is absolutely minimal activity in the main trunk.

From garden center tree to bonsai. This 36 in (90 cm) Beuvronensis pine was bought at a garden center and transplanted immediately into a large seed tray.

This tree will make a good bonsai as it has many low branches, a fairly thick trunk and potentially a good taper.

Branches not wanted should be cut off cleanly using branch pruners.

Choose a fairly robust side branch to serve as the new apex. Cut off the existing apex with a sharp saw as it will be redundant in the design of the bonsai.

Wire the branches with copper or aluminum wire. Ensure that the wire is bound evenly but neither too tightly nor too loosely.

Bend the branches as desired and shape by hand to achieve overall conical form. The tree already looks like a bonsai.

The roots seven months after transplantation. The white fungal mycelium is a sure sign of a healthy tree, now 24 in (60 cm) tall.

The foliage pads will be developed and refined over the next two or three years. I did all this shaping and repotting in just twenty minutes.

Pruning cuts should always be sealed with a tree sealant. Tar-based tree paint is very good for deciduous trees, evergreens respond better to grafting wax, while the Japanese cut-wound paste is fine for both. Vaseline or petroleum jelly is a good substitute for tar paint on deciduous trees.

Shaping

Shaping is very much an aesthetic rather than a mechanical process. It is knowing what to cut that matters. The reader might find the following guidelines useful in this connection.

The first thing to look for in a tree that has potential for bonsai is the main trunk line. This may not always be obvious, especially if a tree has several design possibilities. However, it is important to establish the main trunk line in order to solve the design problem. Unless the main trunk line is delineated, no headway can be made with pruning and shaping. This process also helps establish the front and back of the tree.

Persevere until you have found the main trunk line. If it is not obvious, turn the tree or tilt it through different angles until you see it. The leader will then be one of the main branches of the potential tree. The existing leader often has to be discarded in favor of one of the side branches. When cutting a branch off, do not remove it entirely: Always leave a stump behind in case you want to make a jin from it.

Remember that branches on informal upright trees start from outside the elbow of a bend, and not from the inside of the elbow. Branches normally start from one-third the way up the trunk unless, of course, the trunk is so thick that it does not look odd if they start lower down. The basic shape of the majority of bonsai is triangular, and a tree pruned roughly into a triangular shape will immediately begin to look like a bonsai. Arrange the branches in such a way that each of them can be seen individually. Trees look more convincing if the individual branches are discernible. Trees also look much older if the branches slope downward.

Wiring

The shape of most bonsai trees is created artificially. Even collected trees need some work done to them in order to make them more presentable. The ancient Chinese were able to create magnificent bonsai by the "cut and grow" method, but this can be a painstaking and slow process. The introduction of metal wires has made the modern bonsai artist's work considerably simpler.

Contemporary bonsai enthusiasts find it difficult to imagine how shaping and refinement could have been achieved by the ancient Chinese and Japanese without resorting to wiring. Trees can be made into almost any shape with the aid of wiring but care has to be taken not to break the branches by excessive bending. Either copper or aluminum wire may be used for wrapping round the trunks and branches. As explained before, copper wire should be annealed by burning in a bonfire of newspaper, aluminum wire does not. Aluminum is gradually replacing copper which is more expensive, tends to harden with exposure to the elements and cannot therefore be reused easily. Aluminum wire can be used over and over again without much loss in pliability and because aluminum does not oxidize as easily as copper it is less harmful to bonsai soil. Aluminum wire is also less springy than copper and is therefore better able to set the branches.

How to wire

Good wiring should be evenly spaced and coiled at about 45°.

This wiring is too loose.

Wire of different thicknesses or gauges should be used for wiring different parts of the tree. The thicker the trunk or branch, the heavier the wire should be. If one strand of wire is insufficient to set a branch, use a second one. It is not advisable to use more than two on a branch or trunk as they would look unsightly. Always secure the end of the wire to an anchoring point which may be an adjacent branch or the trunk itself. If the trunk is to be wired, the end of the wire should be inserted into the soil to hold it in place. The length of wire used for a branch or trunk should be 50% longer than the subject to be wired . So if the branch is 8 in (20 cm) long, the length of wire should be 12 in (30cm).

Wire may be wrapped around the tree in either a clockwise or counterclockwise direction; if two or more coils are used on any part of the tree, the direction of coiling must be the same. Wires should never cross in opposing directions as this would hinder sap from flowing freely and could harm the trunk or branch. Although it may seem fairly obvious, it should nevertheless be mentioned that wiring is always started from the thickest part of a trunk or branch working outward to the thinnest part. The wire should always just touch the bark surface, binding it neither too tightly nor too loosely.

The best time to wire is during the early spring just before the buds begin to open. For those who have many trees, this may not always be possible because spring is usually the busiest time of the year. If this is the case, wiring may be done in midwinter. Winter is a very convenient time for wiring deciduous trees as there are no leaves on the branches to contend with. However, wiring can be done at any time of the year. You simply need to know your trees. It normally takes one full growing season to set a branch into its desired position. The wire should therefore be left on for a full growing season in order to obtain the desired result. Even if a particular branch or trunk is to be wired again for a second year in order to establish the set firmly, the current year's wire should be removed and rewound in a slightly different position so as not to mark the bark too deeply. Deep wiring marks or scars are unsightly and can take years to grow out. The best time to remove wire is during the fall. This is especially important for pines because most of the swelling of the branches and trunk occurs in that season.

Wiring that is too close has little effect.

This wiring is too far apart.

Two coils of wire correctly applied to a thick branch or trunk.

Two coils of wire badly attached may strangle the branch.

Try to wire two branches with a single cable only.

Other methods of shaping

Before wire came into vogue, various other methods were used for shaping bonsai. The use of weights (both metal and stone) suspended from branches was one such method. Another common method was to tie down the branches with

The trunk on this Chinese juniper has been wired into an S shape using heavy gauge aluminum wire. A single coil of wire was sufficient to bend the trunk into the desired shape. If, however, one coil of wire proves to be inadequate, a second coil may be wound directly next to the first coil. It is not advisable to use more than two coils of wire on a single branch or trunk.

string attached to the base of the pot or the ground. Trunks were usually shaped by twisting them around metal or wooden rods from a very early age. All these methods are fairly effective, but they are clearly not as good as wiring. The main advantage of wiring is that it is relatively unobtrusive and therefore most acceptable from the aesthetic point of view.

Repotting and root pruning

It is commonly imagined that root pruning is what keeps bonsai small, but this is only part of the secret. Root pruning in itself has no dwarfing effect. The dwarfing process is achieved by a combination of branch and root pruning, coupled with the confinement of the tree in a relatively small pot. A bonsai has to be repotted every so often because the tree soon becomes pot-bound and the only way of keeping it healthy is by teasing out the roots, trimming them and putting the tree back into the

Repotting a tree. Prepare the compost by mixing up equal parts of sharp sand, garden loam, and sphagnum moss peat. Coarse grit can be added to increase drainage.

This field maple has not been repotted for two years but it is certainly ready for repotting now. Depending on the species of tree, repotting may be done from late winter to early summer.

The root ball is teased out with a three-pronged cultivator or fork. The roots should be disentangled and combed out just as one would comb out long hair.

Cut off all the excess roots with a pair of sharp scissors so that the root ball will sit comfortably in the pot with a few inches to spare round the perimeter.

Cover the drainage holes with plastic mesh. In this instance, the same pot is being used as it is still the right shape and size for the tree.

Fill the base of the pot with a $1/2$ in (1cm) of the prepared compost. Some books advocate the use of a layer of grit at the bottom of the pot, but in my view this is not really necessary.

Place the prepared tree in the correct position in its container.

Fill the pot up with compost, making sure that there are no holes. The compost should be pressed down using either fingers or a wooden dibble.

The repotting is complete. Water the tree at once with a watering can and again when the soil begins to dry out. The tree can be put in the open after about three weeks.

same pot with fresh soil. Trimming the roots gives the tree more space in which to grow. The tree is also encouraged to put out finer secondary roots which will in turn induce finer branch and twig formation above the soil. If a bonsai is never repotted or pruned, the roots would soon fill the pot leaving little or no room for air and water, and it would eventually choke itself to death. Repotting at recommended, regular intervals ensures that a tree always has access to adequate air, water, and nutrients through its roots.

Repotting cannot be done at any time of the year. Spring is the ideal time for most varieties. Deciduous trees can be repotted between late winter and early spring (i.e. just before the buds begin to swell). Evergreens benefit from repotting slightly later (i.e. from mid to late spring). Trees are normally repotted just before new growth emerges because this is the time when the cells are most active. Roots and branches pruned at that time have the best chance of renewing themselves.

If the roots are pruned much earlier (e.g. in the middle of winter when the tree is dormant) they might rot. Pruning in the summer has the effect of stopping the supply of water and nutrients to the leaves and branches, causing the tree to wither and die.

Although it is not vital to tease roots apart when transferring a tree into a much larger pot, some teasing and root pruning is always advisable as it stimulates finer root development.

As a general rule, always tease the root ball out first and then cut off the excess roots. Cut away as much root as is necessary so that about a third of the pot can be refilled with fresh soil. After repotting the tree, water it and leave it in a close atmosphere such as a cool greenhouse. It should be watered only sparingly until it begins to show signs of picking up again. This will usually happen after three to four weeks, after which time it can be placed out in the open and watered normally.

The front and back of a tree

Establishing the front and back of a bonsai is the first and most important step in designing a tree. The front should always lean forward slightly, although the apex should never lean beyond the rim of the pot, i.e. if a vertical line is drawn from the apex to the soil this should lie just within the confines of the pot. Although the whole tree should lean forward slightly, the tip of the apex should lean backwards just a fraction. This gives the whole composition a final flourish.

The roots should be evenly spread on both sides of the trunk. The first bend of the trunk should be to the left or to the right but never toward the viewer. It is often easier to establish the back of the tree first—the front is then automatically determined.

Branch disposition

The first branch should preferably start one-third of the way up the trunk. However, this is not a hard and fast rule. For trees which have a very thick trunk, the first branch can start from slightly lower down. Slimmer-trunked trees can have branches which start from much higher up (half-way or even higher). Branches should never be allowed to overhang each other.

Branches which do not get sufficient light will always be sickly and eventually die. For the same reason, the apex should always be kept slightly open so that light can penetrate to the lower branches.

The rear branches of a bonsai should be longer than those at the front or at the side. This is important for both aesthetic and practical reasons because the back branches lend both visual and physical weight to a tree. Because a tree is designed to lean forward slightly, long branches at the front would have an unbalancing effect. Long branches at the back help to create a better perspective.

The preparation of a tree for the workshop

A tree should be kept slightly dry if it is to be pruned, wired, or repotted within the next few days. A dry tree tends to be limp and this makes the various tasks much easier to perform. A "wet" tree on the other hand is more turgid and crisp, and its branches will be more difficult to wire and bend, and any pruning which is done will result in unnecessary bleeding. Teasing the roots from the root ball will also be much more difficult.

This large San Jose juniper was collected from a friend's garden two years ago. It is 40 in (100 cm) high and is about to be shaped into a bonsai. Presently, it has a large trunk 4 in (10 cm) and is growing strongly. It obviously has immense potential as a bonsai, with many driftwood areas

Jinning

To create a jin or driftwood from an ordinary branch, make the initial cut so that it points away from the main trunk. Cut through about one-third of the branch and then rip off the branch by hand or with a pair of pliers, toward the trunk. The action of tearing will leave a more natural finish. Jinned branches on conifers can be treated with lime sulfur straight away; they are best left untreated for at least a year on deciduous trees so that the wood will weather naturally. This gives a much better effect and the wood can be treated after the desired texture has been achieved.

Leaf pruning

Leaf pruning is a process in which the leaves of deciduous trees are removed during the summer thereby forcing the tree to put out a second crop of leaves in the same season. The new leaves are usually smaller in size and the fall color generally better. Although the technique is used in bonsai primarily for the purpose of reducing leaf size, it may also be used as a means of saving a tree which has been badly scorched by the sun. If shrivelled-up leaves were left on a tree, new ones would not grow and the tree would eventually die of starvation because it would not be able to carry on photosynthesis.

Leaf pruning is performed in early or mid-summer—never later. In this process, the leaves are cut off at the leaf stalk with a pair of scissors. The new leaves will emerge after about a fortnight.

Leaf pruning is very debilitating. It should not be performed on trees which have not been growing strongly and, in any case, should not be done on the same tree for two consecutive summers.

Placement of bonsai

Bonsai are, perhaps surprisingly, really outdoor plants and not indoor subjects. It is generally imagined that because bonsai are small they are delicate and therefore need protection from the elements. Nothing could be further from the truth. The trees used for bonsai are more or less hardy forest trees, and would come to more harm indoors than out. While it is true that some bonsai are suitable for growing indoors, these "indoor bonsai" are really only tropical plants that have to be kept indoors during the colder months in order to protect them from the frost. In the tropics they can, of course, be grown in the open.

The creation of driftwood. Make a slanting cut about half-way through the branch, pointing away from the trunk.

Next, snap off the branch where it has been cut and tear it off, pulling toward the trunk so that the broken branch has a rough finish.

For branches over 1 in (2.5 cm) thick, saw the branch off just beyond the point where the jin is supposed to terminate.

The stump is then cut along its length to a depth of about 2 in (5 cm) to form quadrants.

The quadrants on this stump will make the task of jinning easier, since each segment can be removed separately rather than all four at once.

Tear each of the quadrants off in turn using concave branch cutters or long-nosed pliers.

The tearing action is important as it must result in a natural-looking rugged surface.

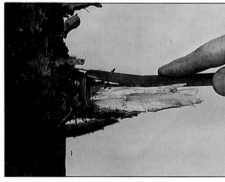

Scrape away the remaining bark and debris using a sharp jinning tool. or if necessary. an ordinary penknife.

The jin should be refined to the desired size and shape using side cutters and a pair of pliers.The wood is always pulled toward the main trunk.

Sometimes it is possible to tear off the pieces of wood by hand.

The jin here is almost complete. As far as possible. avoid using a penknife or craft knife to finish off the jin or driftwood. This would make it look very artificial.

The completed jin can either be treated with lime sulfur straight away, or could be left for a year for the wood to weather naturally before it is applied.

133

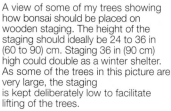

A view of some of my trees showing how bonsai should be placed on wooden staging. The height of the staging should ideally be 24 to 36 in (60 to 90) cm. Staging 36 in (90 cm) high could double as a winter shelter. As some of the trees in this picture are very large, the staging is kept deliberately low to facilitate lifting of the trees.

All bonsai should ideally be kept out of doors. Hence it is best to grow only temperate climate trees in the temperate zone. Bonsai should be placed on some form of staging or bench so that they can be viewed at eye level. Most enthusiasts construct their own staging made from timber. Planks of any size may be used. The ideal height is 3 ft (90 cm). Staging of this height can double as a winter shelter during the colder months when trees need to be protected from the frost. Benches should generally be placed in a fairly sheltered area of the garden, Some benches may be exposed to the full sun while others may be kept in partial shade to cater for the needs of the different varieties of trees.

The use of staging is a good idea for bonsai because the free circulation of air is important for the tree, Bonsai should not, as a rule, stand directly on the ground as the drainage holes can become clogged up and earthworms and pests could enter the soil very easily. Winter protection is best provided by placing trees in a cool greenhouse. Alternatively, trees may be placed under staging which has been covered over with sheets of plastic or old window frames. Deciduous trees may be kept over winter in a frost-free (dark) garden shed but evergreen trees should always be exposed to the light. A cool greenhouse is therefore ideal for evergreens.

Bonsai may also be grown successfully in apartments provided the trees can be placed in the open, such as in a window box or on a balcony. In cities such as London, Paris, Hong Kong, and New York, bonsai enthusiasts keep trees successfully for many years.

Sometimes dead pieces of driftwood can be used very effectively with living trees. The picture at the top is of a dead juniper branch collected from the wild. Beautiful driftwood such as this can be incorporated into bonsai to enhance the look of the tree. The picture on the left shows how a piece has been used in combination with a sapling to create a juniper in the driftwood style. The bark and cambium from one side of the live tree are removed, the live tree is then fastened tightly to the driftwood with either brass nails or string. The development process is a long one, and it could take five or six years before the live tree will callus and grow over the dead driftwood. Patience will be amply rewarded, as the finished tree could look very impressive.

A goat willow (*Salix caprea*) I collected from the wild four years ago and have trained in the driftwood style. The tree was growing in a marsh and the top had rotted away. Except for trimming into an overall conical shape the tree has had very little training. The trunk is the main attraction because of its form, texture, and subtle coloring. Like most willows, this tree is put in a basin of water throughout the summer.

CHAPTER 9

THE BONSAI CALENDAR

January

This is usually the bleakest and coldest month in the temperate zone and there is relatively little that can be done at this time of year. The main task is to protect the trees from the very cold weather. If you have not already put your trees under a winter shelter then this is the time to do so. A cool greenhouse is ideal if you have one, if not build a winter shelter. If your staging is fairly high, at waist level for instance, its top and sides can be draped with heavy-duty polythene to provide some shelter from the cold winds, frost, and snow.

Check that the soil in the pots for those trees which have been under winter shelter since December has not dried out completely. If there are signs of drying out, water the soil so that it is just damp.

In the long winter evenings, start planning your repotting schedule for February. Draw up a list of trees that need repotting and order and buy your peat, grit, and sand according to your compost requirements. Also order any special bonsai pots you need for repotting in the spring.

Nursery trees which have been delivered should be heeled into the ground and not disturbed until late February.

This book has been written from the point of view of the northern hemisphere. For those who live in the southern hemisphere the months corresponding to the various seasons in the northern hemisphere are as shown in the chart below.

	Winter	Spring	Summer	Fall
Northern hemisphere	Dec.Jan.Feb.	Mar. Apr. May	June July Aug.	Sept.Oct. Nov.
Southern hemisphere	June July Aug.	Sept.Oct.Nov.	Dec.Jan.Feb.	Mar. Apr. May

February

This is the start of the repotting season. Begin by mixing a fairly large quantity of the basic bonsai compost (i.e. one-third peat, one-third garden loam or garden compost, one-third sand or grit). Store this in a large plastic bin or under the staging in the cool greenhouse. Add some slow-release fertilizer (about a handful per 5 gallons (25 liters).

During the mild spells toward the end of the month, deciduous trees may be repotted, but it is very important that the newly repotted trees are kept under shelter (e.g. in a cool greenhouse or dry, frost-proof shed). If you intend to lift trees from the ground for potting up later, February is a good time to start. Even if you do not mean to do any lifting until March, this is the right time to begin undercutting the roots. Do not start repotting any of the evergreen trees during February.

Wiring of deciduous trees may be done this month.

Late February is the ideal time for heavy branch pruning of most deciduous trees, except Japanese maples, and most evergreen trees, except pines. Japanese maples are best pruned during late November or early December when the sap has stopped rising. Pruning mountain maples would be a mistake as the sap is rising very rapidly at this time of the year. Pruning of pines is best done in the late summer, i.e. the end of August right through to the end of October, when the sap is rising considerably more slowly. Pruning of pines at this time of the year also gives the tree a better chance to heal.

Any major redesign and reshaping of the trees should be done now.

February is the best month for grafting pines and other evergreens.

If you plan to sow seeds in the spring this is the time to start the stratification process.

March

This is the ideal month for repotting most trees because they are now beginning to show signs of life. Any branch or root pruning done now will heal very quickly, and the trees will therefore be assured of continued vitality. Repotting is best done during the first half of the month. It is a good idea to keep a record of all the trees that have been repotted; you can then calculate when they will next need repotting simply by consulting your records. As a guide, trees less than five years old need to be repotted annually (depending of course on the condition of the root ball); those between five and twenty years old probably need to be repotted every other year; trees over twenty years old about once every three years or so; very old trees such as those approaching one hundred years may not require repotting more than once every four or five years.

By the end of March, trees that have been kept under the staging or in a specially constructed winter shelter can be brought out into the open again. Evergreens may be fertilized using a weak liquid fertilizer at fortnightly intervals. Spray all trees with a fungicide such to kill any remaining spores or mildew and other fungi. Spray also with an insecticide to kill overwintering insects such as greenfly, blackfly, scale insects, and mealybug. Choose a fine, warm day for spraying, and spray during the mid-morning so that the fungicide or insecticide will have a chance to dry.

Sow seeds of deciduous trees which have been stratifying in the refrigerator. If you did not start stratification off last month, there are still another two months to do it because seeds may be sown up to early May.

Wiring and shaping of the trees may be done during this month.

This is probably the last month for lifting trees from the ground. Once the buds on deciduous trees begin to break it is no longer safe to lift them. Evergreens may however continue to be lifted until the end of April.

The end of March and early April is the traditional time for collecting trees from the wild. Trees dug up now have the best chance of survival. They should of course be dug up with as much fibrous root as possible.

April

Many of the operations carried out in March can still be done in April if the weather continues to be rather cool. However, it is probably safer to discontinue all repotting from the middle of April onwards for deciduous trees, and from the end of April for evergreen trees.

Continue with stratification and seed sowing.

Start air-layering evergreens such as junipers, Japanese black and white pines, cryptomeria etc. Deciduous trees that have not been repotted this year should be fertilized from now until the end of summer. Fertilize once a fortnight starting with a weak fertilizer. Never fertilize newly repotted trees until they are well established and growing. This normally takes a couple of months from the time they are repotted. If fertilizer is applied to a freshly repotted tree, the roots can rot. During spring and early summer, a high-nitrogen fertilizer is recommended as this promotes leaf growth. Do not fertilize flowering trees until a couple of months after the flower has fallen. Immediate application of fertilizer will prevent fruit from developing.

This is the best time for taking cuttings of evergreen trees using the previous season's wood. When trimming or thinning out evergreen bonsai such as Hinoki and Sawara cypress, Ezo spruce, and most of the junipers, use the thinnings which have a hard-wood heel for making cuttings. April is the traditional time for house spring cleaning, and this should be extended to bonsai as well. Disinfect the greenhouse after having removed all the plants . The area under the bonsai staging should also be disinfected. If the staging is made of wood, it should be treated with wood preservative. If you use a creosote-based preservative, do not bring plants near the treated wood for at least a fortnight because the fumes will poison the trees.

Start grooming those trees which you wish to show in the summer. By the end of April, spring is very much in the air. All the trees should be putting out new leaves and spring-flowering trees should be starting to bloom.

May

Most deciduous trees should have come into leaf by now and the new candles on pines should be sprouting fast. Continue with the feeding of established trees. Trees still under shelter that were repotted in late February or early March may now be taken out. Watch specimens still in the greenhouse carefully to ensure that they do not dry out completely during very warm spells. Also ensure that the vents in the greenhouse are operating properly and that the temperature in the greenhouse does not rise too high on warm, sunny days.

This is probably the last opportunity for sowing seeds. Seeds sown after the end of May will probably not germinate well. Continue to strike cuttings of evergreen trees.

Start air-layering deciduous trees from the middle of May right through to the end of July. Continue air-layering evergreen trees.

All your trees should now be growing vigorously. Regular watering once a day (preferably in the evening) will be quite essential.

Long shoots of deciduous trees should be pinched back using the thumb and forefinger. Late spring frosts during this month can badly damage the young leaves of deciduous trees, especially the Red maples. Leaves that suffer frost damage will be disfigured for the rest of the year unless, of course, leaf pruning is performed on the trees. If frost is forecast, place the trees which you wish to protect in the greenhouse.

June

In the northern temperate zone, summer really begins in June. This is the month when the days are longest and the temperature begins to rise into the seventies. Watering is by far the most important task during this month. Trees will need to be watered daily in the evening, from 6 pm onwards (unless, of course, it has been raining heavily during the day). On very dry and warm days it may even be necessary to water twice daily—once in the early morning before direct sunlight falls on the trees, and again in the evening.

Apply a granular, organic-based fertilizer, such as dried blood, fish, or bone once a month. Trees will also benefit from a weekly feed of dilute PK fertilizer such as "Phostrogen". So, if you apply a granular fertilizer on the 1st of the month, feed the tree again with a dilute solution of PK fertilizer on the 7th , 14th and 21st of the month before applying granular fertilizer again on the 1st of the following month.

Insect pests such as greenfly and blackfly begin to multiply in June so you should make a regular check of the underside of the leaves and take prompt action the moment they appear.

Continue to make air-layerings of both evergreen and deciduous trees.

June is also the best time for taking soft-wood cuttings. Chinese elm, zelkova, Japanese maple and trident maple cuttings taken in early June will root in three to four weeks under optimum conditions. These rooted cuttings can be potted up individually by the end of July. Seedlings that were sown in March will now have two or three pairs of leaves and may be potted up individually to grow on.

Wiring can, of course, be done throughout the year and there is no reason why it may not continue into June. Take care not to damage the young leaves of deciduous trees.

From the beginning of June until about mid-July, leaf pruning of deciduous trees may be carried out. Maples, beech and sycamore are varieties which are usually leaf pruned in order to induce smaller leaves to develop.

Trees grow very vigorously during this month and constant pinching of the new shoots (including the candles of pines) is essential in order to maintain a good overall shape.

July

Temperatures will rise higher still during July, and watering must continue to be a high priority task. Trees with slightly tender leaves, such as maples and beech, need to be protected from the fierce mid-day sun. They should be moved to a position where they receive only early morning and/or late afternoon sun. If no suitable shade is available in the garden then the construction of overhead shading made of nylon greenhouse netting should be considered.

Continue to look out for insects and other pests and deal with them as quickly as possible in order to prevent their spread. Stick too to your feeding schedule.

Soft-wood cuttings can still be taken but rooted cuttings should not be potted on until the following spring. Cuttings taken in July will root by mid-August or early September, but losses could be high if they are transplanted at this time of the year. Rooted cuttings transplanted during late August or early September will not be able to establish themselves properly to withstand the winter. Continue pinching your trees during July in order to keep them in good shape.

Air-layerings of deciduous trees should have rooted by early July and they should be severed from the parent plant and potted up straight away in pure peat. Keep them in a cool greenhouse for about a month or until the roots completely fill the pot. Fertilizer may be applied now. When the air-layerings appear to be well established they can be taken out of the greenhouse and hardened off in the garden. The same treatment can be applied to the air-layerings of evergreen trees.

August

In a really hot summer, August sunshine can be very harsh indeed. Watering must be done as meticulously as before.

Spray with insecticide as and when pests appear.

From August onwards, trees will need less nitrogen and more potassium and phosphorus to harden the wood and to induce the development of flower and fruit buds. Tomato fertilizer is very good for this purpose.

There is not much to be done now except watering and feeding. If you are planning a vacation during this month and you have a large collection, arrange for a reliable person to water the trees every day. If you have only a few trees, leave them for a friend to look after. Many bonsai enthusiasts never go on vacation during the summer as their trees are too precious to leave. They prefer to holiday in winter instead.

Continue to pot up air-layerings which have put out roots.

Branches start to thicken during August and wire which begins to bite into branches should be loosened.

September

Watering continues to be the most important task during this month. Feeding can be reduced slightly from now on, but it is important to use only a low-nitrogen or nitrogen-free fertilizer.

September is a good month for taking hard-wood cuttings.

This is probably the last opportunity for severing air-layerings that have rooted. After September it would not be advisable to pot up air-layerings as they may not be able to establish sufficient root to withstand the winter. Remove the wires from branches which have set properly. Also keep a close eye on any wired pines because most of the thickening of the branches and trunks occurs during this month.

October

The growing season is now drawing to a close. The deciduous trees are putting on their final splash of color before they shed their leaves. October is a sad month in many ways—but there is still the pleasure of looking at the beautiful fall tints before winter starts to set in. The smell of bonfires fills the evening air and the chore of daily watering will soon be forgotten—from about the middle of the month there will no longer be any need to water.

October is the right time to prune heavy branches on pines as the sap is now no longer rising so rapidly. Pines pruned in fall should be overwintered in a cool greenhouse.

Spray trees with an insecticide and a fungicide to kill overwintering pests and fungus spores. On no account fertilize trees now-they will not need to be fertilized until next March.

November

The deciduous trees will soon, if they have not already done so, lose all their leaves. The evergreens will of course continue to grow, albeit more slowly during the winter months. There is no need to put deciduous trees into their winter shelter until the end of December when the weather begins to turn really cold. Diseased leaves and branches should be burnt in the fall bonfire.

December

Start putting trident and Japanese maples in the cool greenhouse for winter protection. If you do not have one, a wooden frame covered with plastic sheeting is a good substitute. Continue to spray the trees with an insecticide and fungicide on dry, sunny days.

An ancient tomb painting showing a Chinese courtier
with a tray of potted plants.

CHAPTER 10

AESTHETICS

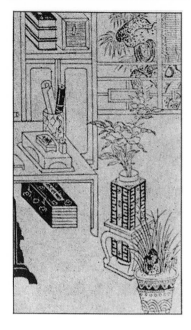

Aesthetics is at the very heart of bonsai and to imagine otherwise is to miss the whole point of what this pastime is all about. While it is true that bonsai cultivation is essentially based on horticulture, the horticultural aspects must not take precedence over the aesthetic factors. A failure to appreciate this point can, and unfortunately often does, result in trees of an abysmally low standard.

Those who neglect aesthetics do bonsai a great disservice. There can never be enough good bonsai. A good-looking tree is always a source of great inspiration to others. Fellow bonsai enthusiasts also use them as models for their own artistic creations. In recent years, there have been some signs of an awakening of aesthetic awareness in the bonsai fraternity and people are beginning to be more discriminating in what they appreciate and buy. In the past, most bonsai enthusiasts devoted almost all their energies to the mechanics of bonsai. Nowadays the balance has shifted slightly in favor of the visual aspects of bonsai design. This of course is the correct approach because bonsai is essentially an art form.

Like any other art form, bonsai can be analyzed, taught, and learnt. The basic principles have a great deal in common with the other visual art forms such as painting and sculpture. The usual limitations to what individuals can achieve apply—great artists after all are born, not made. Most enthusiasts progress to a certain level but no farther. This should be a spur rather than a deterrent though, as much of the pleasure of any pastime is the pursuit of excellence.

The aesthetic principles of bonsai can be learnt in much the same way as any of the other art forms. The aim of this chapter is to give an understanding of how the aesthetic theory should be grafted on to the horticultural practice to make an aesthetically designed tree. Bonsai aesthetics concern line, form, composition, balance, perspective, texture, and color, the same factors governing the visual impressions of the other plastic arts.

Object of bonsai

The object of bonsai is to create a picture or composition using real living trees. Just as in landscape painting where the painter tries to capture a panorama on a small area of canvas, so in bonsai the artist is attempting to reproduce in miniature, with a scale reduction factor of fifty to one hundred, scenery with real trees. The artist's personality and style are usually indelibly stamped on his or her work so that the different styles of different artists are all recognizable to the discriminating.

It has been said that the landscape artist tries to clarify the eternal mystery of the earthly paradise. The bonsai artist tries to clarify the eternal mystery of trees. The analogy between painting and bonsai is an appropriate one. A good painting is

usually one which is personal, fresh, and full of feeling, bold in its perception, sensitive in color, and well proportioned and balanced in its overall composition. The same is true of a good bonsai. If a bonsai has all these qualities then it will certainly qualify as a work of art of the highest order.

How does one achieve good design?

What has just been said about a good painting or a good bonsai is undoubtedly the model of perfection—and therefore unattainable. But there is no point in aiming at second best. To begin with, learn to improvise using ordinary material and let your imagination go. Do not be too rigid or inflexible in your ideas—preconceived ideas and notions of how a tree should be styled are often the biggest stumbling block to creative design. The famous eleventh-century Chinese painter Sun Ti maintained-that landscapes could be seen in the damp patches of the walls of mud huts. So much for imagination! Bonsai artists need to look for beautiful specimen trees in ordinary everyday sources such as collected or garden center material. If a tree will not lend itself to a certain style or design, try to look at it from a completely different angle. The famous bonsai artist John Naka recommends that you bend your mind to suit the tree if it will not bend in the direction you want it to—lateral thinking will not go amiss. This is how new perceptions and vistas are formed.

Two broad groups of factors determine the visual quality of a good bonsai, the aesthetic and the organic, or material factors.

The aesthetic factors are:
(i) The composition of the tree as a whole
(ii) The line and form
(iii) The center of attention
(iv) Balance and harmony
(v) The scale of the composition
(vi) Perspective and depth
(vii) Movement and vitality
(viii) Color
(ix) Texture
The organic factors are:
(i) The trunk
(ii) The branches
(iii) The roots
(iv) The leaves
(v) The fruit and flowers
(vi) The pot or container

Above: Some of the cones may remain on the tree for as long as five or six years.

Left: Collected larch about forty years old and planted on a rock. The tree was collected about fifteen years ago and is now 22 in (55 cm) high. This tree breaks many of the conventional design rules, but its overall composition is extremely pleasing with the rock and the tree together making a delightful picture. The distinctive quality of this particular bonsai is its natural appearance. Most of my larches bear cones regularly because I feed the trees with a high-potash fertilizer during the late summer.

The composition of the tree as a whole

Bear in mind the totality or overall presentation of the bonsai. The overall composition must look natural and resemble a real tree or a real forest. It must above all be pleasing to the eye. Rules need not be strictly observed; they are there to be broken and bonsai may even be the better for it. By breaking the rules, you may introduce a freshness and individuality usually lacking in trees that conform too strictly to the stylistic rules of composition.

This factor is a very important one and cannot be defined or analyzed precisely because it is entirely subjective. The quality of the overall presentation is something which strikes the observer immediately. A tree with good overall presentation stands out, one without it will simply be passed by.

Line and form

Line and form sum up the essence of a bonsai composition. They are to bonsai as contours are to maps. They spell the essential characteristics of a bonsai, and constitute the skeleton or framework around which all the aesthetic elements of a tree are built.

Line can best be defined in terms of the basic style of the tree, e.g. formal upright, informal upright, cascade, and so on. It does not necessarily imply a single line, but more a general drift in a particular direction. Line is important because it channels the eye to the very heart of the composition, and therefore not surprisingly provides a useful method of classification. Line establishes the power and direction of a tree and helps to create an immediate empathy between the observer and the tree. The line of a tree is most powerfully felt in the literati and cascade styles in which the eye naturally runs from base to apex.

Form, on the other hand, is the flesh around the skeleton or framework, and fills in the outline of the tree. The placement of each and every branch, the density of foliage pads and the refinement and ramification are all factors that contribute to the form of the overall composition.

Japanese Black pine (*Pinus thunbergii*) from my collection. This exquisite tree is just over 30 in (80 cm) high and was imported from Japan twenty years ago. It has a very powerful trunk line and immense visual mass. Old trees such as this are not repotted very often; once every four or five years is sufficient. The compost consists of four-parts sharp sand. one-part loam and one-part peat.

The center of attention

An outstanding specimen tree must have something that other trees do not. This is what is known as the "key feature" or main attraction of a particular tree. The key feature transforms an ordinary tree into an extraordinary one. Charisma similarly makes people stand out. Trees which have an outstanding feature attract attention immediately. It may be something as

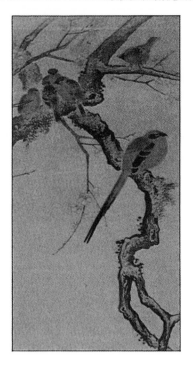

trivial as a twist in the trunk, or as dramatic as a large area of beautiful driftwood. Whatever it is, it will inevitably be the main talking-point. If you see a really spectacular tree, it is perhaps worth analyzing why it is successful. Close analysis will reveal that there is almost certainly one main contributory factor or key element.

The key feature cannot always be contrived. More often than not, it happens more by chance than by design. Driftwood, for example, is normally something which is found on collected trees and cannot usually be successfully created. The really good bonsai artist is able to see the potential for charisma in a tree and must help to bring it out.

Balance and harmony

Balance and harmony imply a sense of equilibrium, a feeling of restfulness. They are in fact the end product of the total creative process.

Whatever the medium, a work of art is incomplete without balance and harmony. One of the great mysteries of life is the ability of the human spirit to discern visual harmony and balance. Like many other phenomena, the perception of harmony and balance cannot be explained. It is probably instinctive and possessed by everyone to varying degrees. Nevertheless, an analysis of how to achieve balance and harmony is possible even if only through the purely negative process of elimination of what does not look right.

Balance and harmony have a great deal to do with the placement and positioning of objects in finite space. In painting, space is two-dimensional, while in bonsai it is three-dimensional. However, the third dimension, i.e.depth, is sometimes regarded as only half a dimension because it is surreal. As in painting, depth and perspective in bonsai can be contrived by visual means.

Considerations of balance and harmony must cover every aspect of bonsai design. Each constituent element of a well-designed tree must "fit" perfectly with every other element. For instance, the different elements of the trunk design such as shape, size, and texture must be in keeping with the rest of the tree. The position of the trunk in relation to the container should be so balanced that it gives a perfect sense of poise. It is possible to go through each and every element of a bonsai (the roots, the trunk, the apex, the side and rear branches etc.) and analyze all the qualities that make for aesthetic harmony.

Scale of composition

Scale is of paramount importance in bonsai design because the primary objective of the artist is to create an illusion of a real

tree. This is where proportion comes in. The proportion of the various elements in relation to one another dictate the overall mood of the tree. Thus, trunk diameter in relation to height can convey the feeling of either a young or an old tree. The height of the first and subsequent branches in relation to the overall height of the tree contribute quite a different part of the overall impression. The sizes of the leaves, flowers, and fruit in relation to the size of the whole tree again convey different moods.

Bonsai do not need to be large physically in order to give the impression of immense size or age. The scale of the various components if skilfully deployed can create the desired impression. An impression of power and grandeur, for instance can be conveyed by the use of thick but relatively short trunks. The foliage pads should be heavy and the roots exposed and gnarled, gripping the soil powerfully. Daintiness and delicacy on the other hand, are conferred in the first place by a slender graceful trunk. The foliage pads should look light and airy and start fairly high up on the trunk. The photographs in Japanese exhibition manuals provide helpful guideiines for classic specimen trees.

Bonsai, of course, come in various sizes and the trend now is to restrict the trunk length, as distinct from trunk height, to 4ft (120 cm). Thus, on an informal upright tree, the length of the trunk, taking in all its curves, should not exceed 4ft (120 cm). As in any of the other visual arts, the very scale of the composition is highly significant. The difference in effect of a miniature and a full-size portrait is comparable to that between tiny and large bonsai. Some bonsai enthusiasts prefer large trees, while others prefer smaller ones. It is purely a matter of personal choice and taste.

Perspective and depth

Bonsai enthusiasts often refer to a bonsai as being convincing when it looks like a real tree. Although this illusion depends on a number of different factors, perspective plays a very important part. Perspective in bonsai is important because the experience of authenticity is a visual one. Perspective and depth are almost synonymous in bonsai because the third dimension, depth, is relatively limited. Depth is best created by having adequate branches at the rear to give visual mass. Scope for applying this principle is rather limited with individual trees, but rather greater when it comes to creating a group or forest planting. You can then use different sizes of trees in very much the same way a landscape painter would. For instance, by placing the smaller trees at the rear you can create the impression of great distance in a relatively shallow depth.

Space is another factor that contributes to perspective and depth. Large areas are often deliberately left empty in group plantings in order to reinforce the scale of the composition. Empty spaces of this kind are often referred to quite wrongly as

"negative areas". They are neither negative nor useless. They are, on the contrary, very positive indeed and serve to enhance those spaces which are filled.

The main attraction of this Chinese juniper (*left, above left and right*) is its beautiful driftwood. The bonsai is well over one hundred years old and only a tiny sliver of live bark remains. This specimen is unusual in that it can be viewed from either side, having no formal front. The tree is 30 in (75 cm) high and has a trunk diameter of 4 in (10 cm). It is planted in a deep rectangular stoneware pot that I made myself.

Movement

Although a bonsai cannot move in the same way that a dancer can, it is nevertheless capable of suggesting movement by the way it has been designed and shaped. Certain bonsai masterpieces have this dynamic quality about them, a certain flow and rhythm. This may be created simply by the sweep of a branch or a slight curve in the trunk; but whatever it is, the tree seems to come alive. This is the quality referred to as movement in a tree.

Color

As in painting, color in bonsai provides the finishing touches to the composition as a whole. Needless to say, color creates

A group of red maples (*Acer palma tum "Chisio"*) grown in a cluster formation. By planting trees together in this way greater perspective is created. Note the subtle shades of pink on the bare branches. The composition has a light and airy feel about it—one could almost say it has movement.

a lasting impression on the viewer. In judging both individual and overall displays of bonsai, color, and texture have a very significant influence on the judges' verdict. If the color is not pleasing, the display as a whole may fail. It is sometimes imagined that a bonsai artist has little or no control over color, but this is not entirely true. Control over color is exerted indirectly by control of the environment in which the bonsai grow, e.g. by the amount and type of fertilizer applied at different times.

Color should not be conceived only in terms of the spectacular, such as a maple is in its full fall glory. If such a tree were grown only for its color, or only for its spectacular flowers, then there would seem to be little point in growing it. If the end objective is simply a brief flash of splendour, the bonsai would be of little or no interest whatsoever for the rest of the year.

Texture

Texture is another important aesthetic consideration in bonsai, and nature provides this in great abundance through the variation in leaf shape and color, branch ramification, and trunk texture.

These factors seem fairly obvious to the more experienced bonsai grower, but they are worth emphasizing in the context of aesthetics. A person viewing a bonsai would normally look at the trunk first (while taking in the overall shape or form of the tree), down at the surface roots, and then up again to the branches and foliage pads and thence to the apex. Any interesting flowers or fruit on the tree would no doubt be noted too.

The trunk

A trunk characterizes a bonsai in the same way that a body characterizes a person. It is the first thing to be noticed. The (bonsai) trunk must have a good taper, narrowing gradually all the way from the base to the apex. A trunk that has no taper will not be convincing, nor will the bonsai be any good. Needless to say, it should lean slightly forward, but not so much as to unbalance the tree.

The roots

A good bonsai should have good surface roots. If a tree has no visible roots it will look like a totem pole rising out of the ground. The roots should be radially spaced round the trunk and those at the front should be particularly pleasing in appearance.

The branches

The branches should normally start from about a third of the way up the trunk. The first branch could be placed either on the left or the right, and the second branch slightly higher up on the opposite side at roughly 120°. The third branch will be at the back to provide the perspective. Branches should continue to be arranged in a radial fashion all the way up to the apex.

The foliage pads

The foliage pads should be well groomed. The leaves or needles should be tightly arranged and all facing upwards. The secondary branches should not start too close to the trunk or

they will clutter up the principal area of interest, which is the trunk itself.

The apex

The apex or crown is an important feature of any bonsai because it gives the finishing touch to the tree. The apex should never be neglected. It should be carefully designed and executed. Some bonsai artists suggest that the apex itself should be designed just like a small bonsai so that it repeats the theme of the main tree.

The fruit and flowers

If a tree is being exhibited mainly for its flowers or fruit then these have to be in prime condition. In bonsai of this sort, each flower or fruit should be very carefully placed so as to produce a good overall balance. In the West, it is not considered good taste to grow bonsai which have flowers and fruit which are completely out of scale with the rest of the tree because this would look unnatural. However, in Japan such trees continue to be very popular.

The pot or container

The choice of container for a bonsai is very much an aesthetic matter, inevitably governed to a large extent by taste and fashion. Deep round pots, for instance, were in vogue a century ago, but today the preference is for much shallower pots. A pot is very much like a picture frame in that its primary purpose is to better define and complement the subject.

The depth of a pot is, as a general rule, determined by the trunk diameter. It is not always an easy principle to follow because trees still in the process of being trained have relatively slim trunks in relation to their height. In any case training pots are larger than the pots used for final display. Tall straight trees look well if planted in shallow rectangular or oval pots.

Dainty trees will gain extra elegance if planted in shallow round or oval pots while bulkier trees, on the other hand, look best in correspondingly deeper and heavier pots.

Windswept trees are enhanced by pots that reinforce their ruggedness, and modern ceramic pots are therefore very suitable.

Literati trees are traditionally planted in round incurve pots, but there is really no reason why they cannot be planted in modern pots.

A group planting of seven Sawara cypress
(*Chamaecvparis pisifera* "Boulevard").

CHAPTER 11

SHOWING AND JUDGING

As you become more proficient in the art of bonsai, you may naturally wish to display your trees in public. In most countries there is usually ample opportunity for this at horticultural shows and other special exhibitions. During the summer there are numerous local, regional, and national flower shows where exhibits of bonsai are frequently seen. At these shows, both individuals and clubs may exhibit their trees. Enquiries for exhibiting should be made to the organization sponsoring the show. The organizers are generally very helpful and will be able to provide information on the conditions for exhibiting bonsai. Local and regional horticultural shows are, of course, much easier to enter than the more important national ones.

Most bonsai clubs also hold their own shows from time to time, and members should take every opportunity to show their trees on these occasions. This gives pleasure not only to exhibitors but also to visitors. Above all, it will help to develop your confidence in exhibiting bonsai.

Trees intended for exhibition and display need to be groomed so that they look their very best. If you are taking the trouble to show at all, it is worth making the extra effort to put on the best display possible. Trees for exhibition must be in prime condition. Evergreen trees should look fresh and green, and deciduous trees should have the appropriate leaf color for the particular time of year. The trunks and branches must be clean, and if there are areas of driftwood they should be reasonably clean as well. Exhibitors occasionally apply lime sulfur to driftwood areas just before a show in order to highlight the deadwood. However, this is not a good practice as the freshly painted wood could make a tree look very artificial. It is better to apply the lime sulfur a couple of months before the show so that the driftwood looks weathered and more natural.

In the past, trees with wire on their branches were never shown at exhibitions because they were regarded as trees still in the process of being trained. This convention is now gradually being disregarded because fine trees can still be very presentable even if some branches are wired. Moreover, the use of copper or anodized aluminum wire can be quite unobtrusive.

The pots in which the trees are displayed should, of course, be clean and the tree and pot together should, if possible, be displayed on a proper bonsai stand. These stands need not be antique stands-these are difficult to obtain anyway. Some fine reproduction stands, or even home-produced stands, are just as effective. A bonsai stand somehow always completes the picture and is part of the overall presentation of a bonsai. One famous Chinese bonsai master has compared a bonsai to a beautiful lady. The tree is the lady herself, the pot is her general attire, and the stand her shoes. Exhibiting a bonsai without a stand is very much like a lady appearing in public without any shoes.

Accent or accessory plantings in small bonsai pots

are also part of the traditional way of displaying bonsai. They are intended to complement or contrast with the main bonsai exhibits. The accent plantings act as a foil to the much larger main trees. They are usually small plantings of grass, fern, or bamboo. Sometimes an accent planting may even be a small tree or a rock. To be effective, it needs to be both small and at the same time dainty.

When putting on a display of bonsai, several trees will invariably be needed and the exhibit must be designed as a unified whole. It is not sufficient to have good individual trees if the overall effect is confusing and incoherent. The way each tree leans, the leaf colors, shapes, and sizes must all blend and complement one another. The background for the display should be neutral so that it does not detract from the trees themselves; colors such as gray, powder-blue, light pink, very light mauve, buff, and off-white are suitable. Similarly, the surface on which the trees stand needs to be neutral too. Neutral-colored felt or hessian are suitable for both the backdrop and the table surface. Gravel, sand, vermiculite, or rush matting all provide effective surfaces for displaying bonsai. Avoid using too many artifacts such as lanterns and other japanese ornaments in the display as they can clutter up the stand and detract from the trees. Allow adequate space between them so that each one's individual beauty and charm can be appreciated to the full. Too many trees in a display can be a recipe for disaster.

At major bonsai exhibitions in japan, the tables are covered with dark blue felt and the background is pale yellow or straw-colored board. Spotlights are used to highlight the trees. As many as five hundred to one thousand major trees may be featured at such exhibitions. The premier bonsai exhibition in japan is the National Bonsai Exhibition or "Kokufu Ten" which is held each spring at the Tokyo Metropolitan Art Museum in Ueno Park. At this particular exhibition two hundred to three hundred trees are usually displayed.

In Britain the premier flower show is the Royal Horticultural Society's Chelsea Flower Show which is held in the last week of May. In recent years there have been as many as nine separate stands of bonsai.

Bonsai are also appropriately being increasingly exhibited in art galleries.

As a bonsai exhibitor, you should bear in mind that the public like variety. They like to see trees of different ages on display. The daintiness of a small *mame* can be just as fascinating as the grandeur of a two-hundred-year-old tree. Your stand should also have a good mix of color in the foliage. Listed below are some of the factors that judges ought to be looking for in the overall display of a bonsai exhibit.

Suggested system for judging a bonsai stand

Aspect being judged	Maximum points
1 Overall impression (i.e. trees and stand seen as a whole)	20
2 Quality and condition of individual exhibits (i.e. health and beauty of plants)	35
3 Color, variety, and texture of exhibits	20
4 Attention to detail	5
5 Quality of staging, staging material and accessories	10
6 Uniqueness or special features which deserve special recognition	10
Total points	100

However, when it comes to judging the merits of individual trees, quite different considerations come into play. The following are some of the factors which judges should be looking for when judging individual specimens.

Suggested system for judging an individual bonsai tree

Feature	Maximum points
1 Trunk (a) Shape	10
(b) Taper	5
(c) Bark texture/color	5
2 Branches (a) Position on trunk	10
(b) Shape	5
(c) Density	5
3 Roots	10
4 Overall shape of tree	10
5 Health and condition	5
6 Suitability of pot/container	5
7 Position of tree in pot/containter	5
8 Attention to detail	10
9 Overall artistic interpretation	15
Total points	100

Overall shape of tree

Attention to detail

Branches

Trunk

Health and condition

Roots

Suitability of container

Position of bonsai in container

Overall artistic interpretation

This beautiful little cotoneaster planted against a rock
is only 10 in (25 cm) high. It was developed from a tree
growing in my front garden fifteen years ago. The scar
on the trunk was caused by mower damage. The tree is
probably about twenty-five to thirty years old. The bonsai is
very Chinese in character, with extensive use of rocks.

CHAPTER 12

THE INTERNATIONAL SCENE

I am training this very tall Sawara cypress bonsai for the Federation of British Bonsai Societies' logo competition. It is 48 in (120 cm) high and has a trunk diameter of nearly 3 $\frac{1}{4}$ in (8 cm). It was created from a nursery tree just six months before this photograph was taken. The tree is by no means perfect, but it already bears a striking resemblance to the logo.

Although bonsai has been practised by the Japanese for the last nine-hundred years, and by the Chinese for even longer, it was not until the turn of the twentieth century that bonsai first found its way into Europe. Early European traders and missionaries would no doubt have come across some of these curious little trees in the seventeenth and eighteenth centuries, but none took a keen interest in them. Even the famous European plant hunters of the eighteenth century paid scant attention to them.

The first public exhibition of bonsai in the West was probably in London in 1909. Some enterprising merchants may have imported a few bonsai into Britain from China and Japan around about this time, but they were never exactly popular. Bonsai were invariably regarded as curiosities more than anything else. Chinese and Japanese flower pots on the other hand were imported on a relatively large scale. The fact that there are still so many of them to be found in antique shops is fair evidence of their popularity.

Bonsai did not catch on in a big way in the UK until after the Second World War. By the mid-1950s quite a number of people in Britain were beginning to show interest. This increased during the 1960s and mushroomed in the 1970s. The first-ever public

I created this massive San Jose juniper under the guidance of the great bonsai master John Naka. This photograph was taken just five months after the tree was styled. The tree was allowed to grow vigorously in summer in order to develop a more prominent apex. It w ill be shaped again in the following spring to reflect John Naka's original design more closely.

display of bonsai at the Chelsea Flower Show was in 1962. Today in Britain there are nearly forty clubs which cater for bonsai enthusiasts, and a national organization, called the Federation of Bonsai Societies, was set up in 1981 to coordinate the activities of the various clubs. The first-ever National Bonsai Convention was held in 1981, and the second in 1983.

Interest in bonsai in Europe is even more recent. During the 1960s, there was hardly any interest at all in bonsai but since the early 1970s the following has increased rapidly. Today in most western European countries there are bonsai shops and nurseries, and numerous clubs which cater for the enthusiast. Most, if not all, the pots and trees are imported from Japan and China. Only a very few bonsai are made locally.

In the United States, the development of bonsai has been greatly influenced and helped by the Japanese immigrant community on the West coast. In California particularly there are many very good bonsai clubs where Japanese bonsai masters are to be found. The interest in bonsai in the United States is probably stronger than in any other country outside Japan and China. There is significant interest too in bonsai in Australia, South

A bonsai stretcher of the kind shown here is extremely useful for moving heavy and awkward trees around the garden or at bonsai shows. The tree is a partly trained Beuvronensis pine in a 26 by 18 in (65 by 45 cm) pot. The stretcher makes carrying it just that little easier.

Africa, India, Argentina, Canada, Chile, Spain, Austria, Switzerland, Korea, Thailand, and Indonesia, not to mention the originating countries of China and Japan.

Public exhibitions and displays of bonsai are becoming increasingly popular. These exhibitions certainly promote great interest in bonsai, and the public generally finds them very attractive and enjoyable. Bonsai enthusiasts are usually introduced to bonsai through public exhibitions such as these, which therefore serve a very useful purpose.

Clubs also organize special outings and visits to bonsai gardens and nurseries from time to time. They may also run useful courses on various specialized aspects of bonsai. For those who cannot attend club meetings regularly, club magazines and journals can also be very useful as a source of information.

Bonsai in Japan

Bonsai is, of course, big business in Japan. Thousands of nurseries there grow bonsai for export to the West and for the home market. They are centered mostly on Tokyo in the Omiya region. However, there are also a few nurseries in other parts of Japan. These nurseries are usually small family businesses and the expertise is passed down from one generation to the next. The export trade is usually organized through a sophisticated system of agents who scout around the various nurseries to match the requirements of customers with the availability of trees. If a client wants a particular species of tree in a particular style and of a certain age, the agent will look around to find a tree of that description.

The bonsai pot industry is also a very large and well organized one. These potteries are usually family businesses and are often highly mechanized. The quality of Japanese pots

is very high. They are usually made of stoneware, although some porcelain pots are still made. There is also a thriving business in tools, wire, and the other bonsai accessories.

The premier organization for bonsai in Japan is the Nippon Bonsai Association which promotes many bonsai activities, including the prestigious Koko Fu Exhibition which is held annually in Osaka in the spring. Besides the Nippon Bonsai Association, there are also various growers' and producers' associations which are trade associations for the promotion of bonsai.

Left and above: Japanese lanterns like these add an Asian touch to the garden. No bonsai display area would be complete without one. The lantern on the left is 60 in (150 cm) tall and is made from reconstituted stone. Moss is encouraged to grow on it by standing it under trees. The lantern on the right about 36 in (90 cm) is made from sandstone and was imported from Japan.

Bonsai in China

In the West very little is known about the contemporary bonsai scene in China because the country has been virtually closed to the outside world for nearly three decades. Now that visitors are able to travel there more freely, information is becoming increasingly available about the state of the art there. Reports happily confirm that the Chinese style of bonsai is different from the Japanese style: such diversity enriches rather than detracts from the art of bonsai generally.

In China there are many centers where bonsai are grown. The most famous of these are in Guangzhow in Guang Dong Province; Shanghai; Chengdu, in Sichuan Province; and Suzhou and Yangzhou in Jiangsu Province. The different areas specialize in different species of trees and have their own distinctive styles. The growers in Guangzhou, for instance, represent the Southern school or Lingnan School of bonsai. In Shanghai there is a famous botanical garden which has a very large collection of potted trees from all the various parts of China.

The Chinese are very fond of flowers and plants, and many floral exhibitions are held throughout the country around the Chinese New Year. These exhibitions invariably feature bonsai. Those who have visited Hong Kong (China) will be familiar with the bonsai from China which are exhibited there at about the same time. There are also permanent exhibitions of potted trees in many public parks in China for the public to admire.

Because bonsai are considered to be beautiful objects they are used extensively in China for decorating parks, public buildings, hotel rooms, restaurants, and even trains.

In the last few years, a number of Chinese nurseries have begun to export their trees to the West, and a variety of Chinese bonsai can now be purchased in bonsai shops and nurseries throughout Europe. Bonsai pots from China are also being exported in large quantities.

The National Bonsai Association of China was formed in Beijing in December 1981.

Above left and above: There are many designs of Japanese lantern .Some of them are extremely simple and easy to make. The one shown here can be made very simply using six individual pieces of ordinary concrete. The picture on the right shows how basic the design is; yet the lantern is very attractive.

INDEX

A